Uncover 3 Student's Book

Ben Goldstein • Ceri Jones
with **Susan Banman Sileci**

CAMBRIDGE
UNIVERSITY PRESS

University Printing House, Cambridge CB2 8BS, United Kingdom

One Liberty Plaza, 20th Floor, New York, NY 10006, USA

477 Williamstown Road, Port Melbourne, VIC 3207, Australia

314–321, 3rd Floor, Plot 3, Splendor Forum, Jasola District Centre, New Delhi – 110025, India

79 Anson Road, #06–04/06, Singapore 079906

Cambridge University Press is part of the University of Cambridge.

It furthers the University's mission by disseminating knowledge in the pursuit of education, learning and research at the highest international levels of excellence.

www.cambridge.org
Information on this title: www.cambridge.org/9781107493407

© Cambridge University Press 2015

This publication is in copyright. Subject to statutory exception and to the provisions of relevant collective licensing agreements, no reproduction of any part may take place without the written permission of Cambridge University Press.

First published 2015

20

Printed in Great Britain by CPI Group (UK) Ltd, Croydon CR0 4YY

A catalog record for this publication is available from the British Library.

ISBN 978-1-107-49340-7 Student's Book 3
ISBN 978-1-107-49342-1 Student's Book with Online Workbook and Online Practice 3
ISBN 978-1-107-49347-6 Teacher's Book 3
ISBN 978-1-107-49345-2 Workbook with Online Practice 3
ISBN 978-1-107-49352-0 Presentation Plus Disc 3
ISBN 978-1-107-49348-3 Class Audio CDs (3) 3
ISBN 978-1-107-49350-6 Video DVD 3

Additional resources for this publication at www.cambridge.org/uncover

The publishers have no responsibility for the persistence or accuracy of URLs for external or third-party Internet websites referred to in this publication, and do not guarantee that any content on such websites is, or will remain, accurate or appropriate. Information regarding prices, travel timetables and other factual information given in this work is correct at the time of first printing but Cambridge University Press does not guarantee the accuracy of such information thereafter.

Art direction, book design, photo research, and layout services: QBS Learning
Audio production: John Marshall Media

Acknowledgments

Many teachers, coordinators, and educators shared their opinions, their ideas, and their experience to help create *Uncover*. The authors and publisher would like to thank the following people and their schools for their help in shaping the series.

In Mexico:
María Nieves Maldonado Ortiz (Colegio Enrique Rébsamen); Héctor Guzmán Pineda (Liceo Europeo); Alfredo Salas López (Campus Universitario Siglo XXI); Rosalba Millán Martínez (IIPAC [Instituto Torres Quintero A.C.]); Alejandra Rubí Reyes Badillo (ISAS [Instituto San Angel del Sur]); José Enrique Gutiérrez Escalante (Centro Escolar Zama); Gabriela Juárez Hernández (Instituto de Estudios Básicos Amado Nervo); Patricia Morelos Alonso (Instituto Cultural Ingles, S.C.); Martha Patricia Arzate Fernández, (Colegio Valladolid); Teresa González, Eva Marina Sánchez Vega (Colegio Salesiano); María Dolores León Ramírez de Arellano, (Liceo Emperadores Aztecas); Esperanza Medina Cruz (Centro Educativo Francisco Larroyo); Nubia Nelly Martínez García (Salesiano Domingo Savio); Diana Gabriela González Benítez (Colegio Ghandi); Juan Carlos Luna Olmedo (Centro Escolar Zama); Dulce María Pascual Granados (Esc. Juan Palomo Martínez); Roberto González, Fernanda Audirac (Real Life English Center); Rocio Licea (Escuela Fundación Mier y Pesado); Diana Pombo (Great Union Institute); Jacobo Cortés Vázquez (Instituto María P. de Alvarado); Michael John Pryor (Colegio Salesiano Anáhuac Chapalita)

In Brazil:
Renata Condi de Souza (Colégio Rio Branco); Sônia Maria Bernal Leites (Colégio Rio Branco); Élcio Souza (Centro Universitário Anhaguera de São Paulo); Patricia Helena Nero (Private teacher); Célia Elisa Alves de Magalhães (Colégio Cruzeiro-Jacarepaguá); Lilia Beatriz Freitas Gussem (Escola Parque-Gávea); Sandra Maki Kuchiki (Easy Way Idiomas); Lucia Maria Abrão Pereira Lima (Colégio Santa Cruz-São Paulo); Deborah de Castro Ferroz de Lima Pinto (Mundinho Segmento); Clara Vianna Prado (Private teacher); Ligia Maria Fernandes Diniz (Escola Internacional de Alphaville); Penha Aparecida Gaspar Rodrigues (Colégio Salesiano Santa Teresinha); Silvia Castelan (Colégio Santa Catarina de Sena); Marcelo D'Elia (The Kids Club Guarulhos); Malyina Kazue Ono Leal (Colégio Bandeirantes); Nelma de Mattos Santana Alves (Private teacher); Mariana Martins Machado (Britannia Cultural); Lilian Bluvol Vaisman (Curso Oxford); Marcelle Belfort Duarte (Cultura Inglesa-Duque de Caxias); Paulo Dantas (Britannia International English); Anauã Carmo Vilhena (York Language Institute); Michele Amorim Estellita (Lemec – Lassance Modern English Course); Aida Setton (Colégio Uirapuru); Maria Lucia Zaorob (CEL-LEP); Marisa Veiga Lobato (Interlíngua Idiomas); Maria Virgínia Lebrón (Independent consultant); Maria Luiza Carmo (Colégio Guilherme Dumont Villares/CEL-LEP); Lucia Lima (Independent consultant); Malyina Kazue Ono Leal (Colégio Bandeirantes); Debora Schisler (Seven Idiomas); Helena Nagano (Cultura Inglesa); Alessandra de Campos (Alumni); Maria Lúcia Sciamarelli (Colégio Divina Providência); Catarina Kruppa (Cultura Inglesa); Roberto Costa (Freelance teacher/consultant); Patricia McKay Aronis (CEL-LEP); Claudia Beatriz Cavalieri (By the World Idiomas); Sérgio Lima (Vermont English School); Rita Miranda (IBI – [Instituto Batista de Idiomas]); Maria de Fátima Galery (Britain English School); Marlene Almeida (Teacher Trainer Consultant); Flávia Samarane (Colégio Logosófico); Maria Tereza Vianna (Greenwich Schools); Daniele Brauer (Cultura Inglesa/AMS Idiomas); Allessandra Cierno (Colégio Santa Dorotira); Helga Silva Nelken (Greenwich Schools/Colégio Edna Roriz); Regina Marta Bazzoni (Britain English School); Adriano Reis (Greenwich Schools); Vanessa Silva Freire de Andrade (Private teacher); Nilvane Guimarães (Colégio Santo Agostinho)

In Ecuador:
Santiago Proaño (Independent teacher trainer); Tania Abad (UDLA [Universidad de Las Americas]); Rosario Llerena (Colegio Isaac Newton); Paúl Viteri (Colegio Andino); Diego Maldonado (Central University); Verónica Vera (Colegio Tomás Moro); Mónica Sarauz (Colegio San Gabriel); Carolina Flores (Colegio APCH); Boris Cadena, Vinicio Reyes (Colegio Benalcázar); Deigo Ponce (Colegio Gonzaga); Byron Freire (Colegio Nuestra Señora del Rosario)

The authors and publisher would also like to thank the following contributors, script writers and collaborators for their inspired work in creating *Uncover*:
Anna Whitcher, Janet Gokay, Kathryn O'Dell, Lynne Robertson, Dana Henricks

Unit	Vocabulary	Grammar	Listening	Conversation (Useful language)
1 Life on the Edge pp. 2–11	■ Extreme weather ■ Basic needs	■ Simple present and present continuous review ■ Simple past and past continuous review ■ *used to* Grammar reference p. 106	■ Biking the Pan-American Highway	■ Agreeing and disagreeing
2 First Things First! pp. 12–21	■ Priorities ■ Emotions	■ *have to/don't have to* ■ *must* ■ Modals of obligation – *should, ought to, had better* ■ *It's* + adjective + infinitive Grammar reference p. 107	■ Take it easy!	■ Helping someone to do something
3 Art All Around Us pp. 22–31	■ Visual arts ■ Musical instruments	■ Verb + *-ing* form (gerund) review ■ *-ing* forms (gerunds) as subjects ■ Verbs + prepositions + *-ing* forms (gerunds) Grammar reference p. 108	■ Leo the one-man band	■ Inviting a friend and arranging to meet
4 Sign Me Up! pp. 32–41	■ Adventure travel ■ Phrasal verbs related to travel	■ Present perfect with *already, yet*, and *just* ■ Present perfect questions ■ Present perfect with *for* and *since* ■ *How long . . . ?* and the present perfect Grammar reference p. 109	■ Adventure travel experiences	■ Signing up for an adventure activity
5 Yikes! pp. 42–51	■ Fears ■ *-ed* and *-ing* adjective endings	■ Future review – *will, be going to*, present continuous ■ First conditional ■ Modals of probability – *must, can't, may, might, could* Grammar reference p. 110	■ Conversations at an amusement park	■ Expressing disbelief

Unit 1–5 Review Game pp. 52–53

Writing	Reading	Video	Accuracy and fluency	Speaking outcomes
■ A persuasive email	■ *Freezing in Siberia* ■ Reading to write: *A fun vacation* ■ Culture: *Tristan da Cunha*	■ *The Long Winter* ■ *Which do you prefer, towns and cities or the country?* ■ *An Island Flood* ■ *The Khomani San of the Kalahari* (CLIL Project p. 116)	■ Not using *a* to talk about the weather ■ Pronunciation of *used to*	I can . . . ■ talk about extreme weather. ■ discuss how my environment affects my life. ■ talk about past incidents and habits. ■ ask for agreement. ■ discuss a faraway place.
■ A blog post about solving a problem	■ *Getting Some Shut-Eye* ■ Reading to write: *Stories of Stress* ■ Culture: *Ten Things I Bet You Didn't Know About . . . Cheerleading*	■ *Get Up and Go!* ■ *What makes a good friend?* ■ *Irish Dancing*	■ Using *to* after *ought*, *should*, and *had better* ■ The letter *c*	I can . . . ■ discuss my priorities. ■ express obligation and prohibition. ■ make strong recommendations. ■ offer help to someone. ■ discuss a sport or cultural activity.
■ A blog post about a concert	■ *Everyone's an Artist* ■ Reading to write: *Fantastic Free Concert* ■ Culture: *A Temporary Desert City*	■ *Original Art* ■ *Have you ever been to a concert?* ■ *A World of Music* ■ *Art in Perspective* (CLIL Project p. 117)	■ Using the *-ing* form after *enjoy* ■ Word stress with *love* and *hate* ■ Spelling the *-ing* forms	I can . . . ■ talk about visual arts. ■ express my likes and dislikes. ■ discuss music. ■ make invitations and arrangements. ■ discuss a cultural event.
■ An email comparing different customs	■ *Anchors Aweigh!* ■ Reading to write: *Tipping help!* ■ Culture: *Five Good Reasons to Visit New Zealand*	■ *The Age of Discovery* ■ *What's the most exciting thing you've ever done?* ■ *Fun in Australia*	■ Using *go* before activities that end in *-ing* ■ Word stress with time words	I can . . . ■ talk about adventure travel. ■ ask and answer questions about personal experiences. ■ ask and answer questions about the duration of activities. ■ talk about signing up for an adventure activity. ■ discuss reasons to visit a place.
■ An email to a friend about plans and problems	■ *Ask Maria* ■ Reading to write: *Afraid to fly!* ■ Culture: *Superstitions? Who needs them?!*	■ *Creepy Creatures* ■ *What are you afraid of?* ■ *Calendars of the Ancient Maya* ■ *City vs. Country* (CLIL Project p. 118)	■ Pronunciation of *I'll* as /al/ ■ Not using *must* for future probability	I can . . . ■ identify and discuss common fears. ■ talk about future events. ■ talk about things that are possible and not possible. ■ express disbelief. ■ discuss superstitions.

Unit	Vocabulary	Grammar	Listening	Conversation (Useful language)
6 Difficult Decisions pp. 54–63	■ School life ■ Expressions with *make* and *do*	■ Second conditional ■ Second conditional *yes/no* questions ■ Second conditional *Wh-* questions Grammar reference p. 111	■ Would you tell the teacher?	■ Asking for and giving advice
7 Smart Planet pp. 64–73	■ Materials ■ Eco-construction verbs	■ Simple present passive ■ Infinitives of purpose ■ Simple past passive Grammar reference p. 112	■ Tour of a museum EcoHouse	■ Apologizing
8 Run for Cover! pp. 74–83	■ Natural disasters ■ Survival essentials	■ Past perfect ■ Past perfect *yes/no* questions ■ Past perfect and simple past Grammar reference p. 113	■ Survival story	■ Explaining a personal problem
9 He Said, She Said pp. 84–93	■ Reporting verbs ■ Communication methods	■ Quoted speech vs. reported speech ■ Reported questions Grammar reference p. 114	■ Short conversations	■ Comparing different accounts of a story
10 Don't Give Up! pp. 94–103	■ Goals and achievements ■ Emotions related to accomplishments	■ Reflexive pronouns ■ Reflexive pronouns with *by* ■ Causative *have/get* Grammar reference p. 115	■ Challenging situations	■ Reassuring someone

Unit 6–10 Review Game pp. 104–105

Writing	Reading	Video	Accuracy and fluency	Speaking outcomes
An article about online safety	*A School with a Difference* Reading to write: *How to Be Safe Online!* Culture: *Punishment or Rehabilitation?*	*Working Together* *Who would you talk to if you needed advice?* *Watch Your Identity*	Pronunciation of /ʊ/ and /u/ Using the simple past after *if* in the second conditional	I can . . . talk about school life. talk about good and bad behavior at school and home. discuss difficult situations. ask for and give advice. discuss different systems for dealing with crime.
A newspaper article about an event	*Houses Made of Garbage* Reading to write: *Volunteers Clean Valley Nature Reserve* Culture: *Under the Australian Sun*	*Where Does it All Go?* *What kind of volunteer work can you do in your school or town?* *Build It Better* *Driving into the Future* (CLIL Project p. 119)	Including *is* or *are* in passive sentences	I can . . . identify materials. talk about how people recycle and reuse materials. talk about eco-construction. apologize. discuss solar energy and sun safety.
A story about a personal experience	*Krakatoa* Reading to write: *Story Source* Culture: *It isn't just a hobby.*	*Land of Volcanoes* *Do you often lose things?* *Storm Chasers*	Pronunciation of /æ/ and /ɒ/ Using the past perfect for events completed before another past moment	I can . . . discuss natural disasters. ask and answer questions about past experiences. discuss past events. ask about and discuss personal problems. discuss tornadoes and people who chase tornadoes.
An essay about social networking sites	*Communication Changes* Reading to write: *Are Cell Phones Good for Teenagers?* Culture: *The World Speaks One Language*	*Social Networks* *What do you think about celebrity gossip?* *The Language of the Future?* *Pictures with Meaning* (CLIL Project p. 120)	Pronunciation of final consonants /d/, /l/, /m/, and /n/ Not using *do* in reported questions	I can . . . talk about different ways of speaking. discuss social networking. talk about different communication methods. compare stories. discuss language use throughout the world.
A personal action plan	*Make Your Dreams Come True* Reading to write: *Achieving My Goal* Culture: *Olympics for the Brain*	*Lifeguard and Athlete* *Have you ever given a class presentation?* *Circus Star*	The sound /i:/ in words with the letters *ie* and *ei* Consonant clusters Getting/having something done	I can . . . talk about goals and accomplishments. discuss emotions related to accomplishments. discuss steps toward achieving goals. reassure someone. discuss an academic competition.

Irregular verbs p. 121

1 Life on the Edge

Discovery EDUCATION

BE CURIOUS

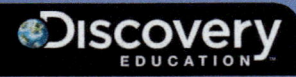

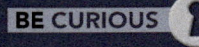

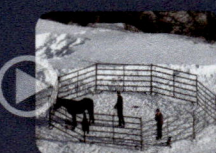

The Long Winter

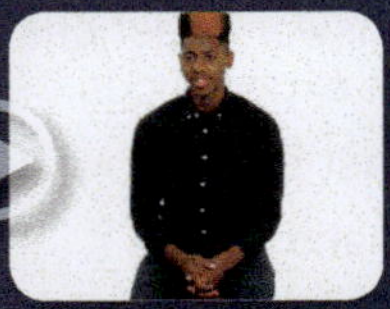

Which do you prefer – towns and cities or the country?

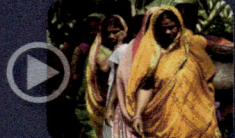

An Island Flood

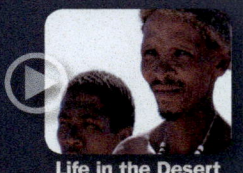

Life in the Desert

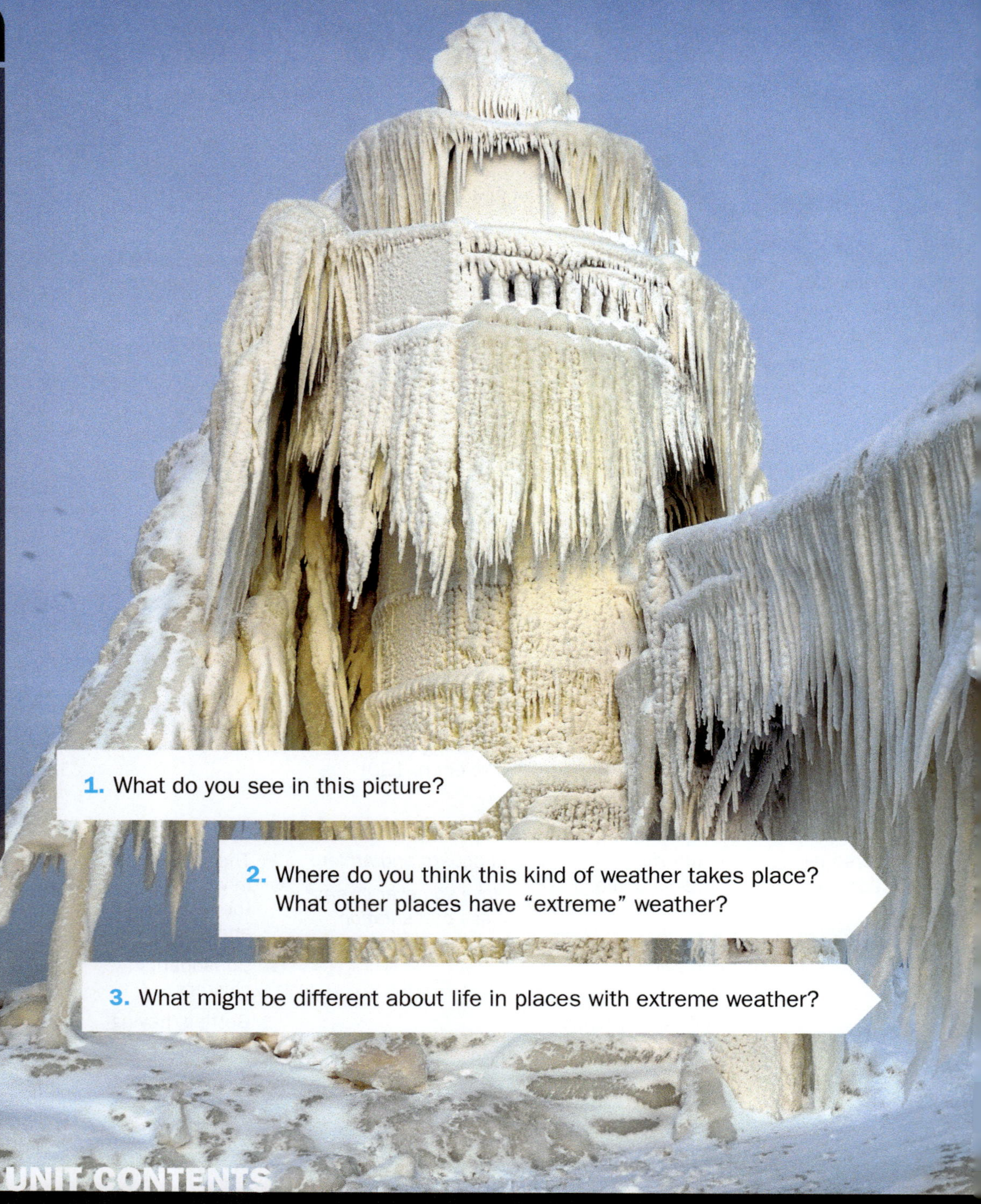

1. What do you see in this picture?
2. Where do you think this kind of weather takes place? What other places have "extreme" weather?
3. What might be different about life in places with extreme weather?

UNIT CONTENTS

Vocabulary Extreme weather; basic needs

Grammar Simple present and present continuous review; simple past and past continuous review

Listening Biking the Pan-American Highway

Vocabulary: Extreme weather

1. Match the words and phrases with the correct pictures.

1. _g_ high winds
2. ___ blizzard
3. ___ hail
4. ___ heat wave
5. ___ thunder and lightning
6. ___ heavy rain
7. ___ fog

 2. Listen, check, and repeat.

3. Which of the words and phrases in Exercise 1 do you associate with a) very hot weather, b) very cold weather, c) hot or cold weather?

→ **Get it RIGHT!**
Don't use the article *a* to talk about weather.
Yakutsk has **very cold** weather.
NOT: ~~Yakutsk has **a very cold** weather.~~

4. Think about where you live. When do you experience extreme weather? Write the words and phrases from Exercise 1 in the following categories.

Sometimes in the summer	Sometimes in the winter	At least once a month	Only once or twice a year	Never

Speaking: What's it like outside?

5. **YOUR TURN** Work with a partner. Ask and answer the questions.
1. What other words do you know to describe weather?
2. What's the weather like today where you live?
3. What weather stories are in the news right now?

6. Talk to your partner about the weather where you live.

> We're having a bad heat wave this week. Right now it's 35°C!

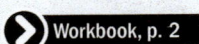 Workbook, p. 2

Reading Freezing in Siberia!; A fun vacation; Tristan da Cunha
Conversation Agreeing and disagreeing
Writing A persuasive email

The COLDEST TOWN on EARTH

Freezing in Siberia!

Yakutsk – the coldest town on Earth. From November to March, it's only light for three or four hours a day, and the temperature is hardly ever above freezing. The average daytime temperature is –30°C, and at night, it sometimes falls as low as –60°C. Now that's cold!

Right now, I'm writing on my computer in the library. It's warm inside, but outside, people are wearing heavy pants, tall boots, hats, scarves, and heavy coats. It often takes me half an hour to get ready to leave the house. When I get home, it takes me another half an hour to take off all those clothes!

Life in the extreme cold is difficult. At –20°C, the air freezes inside your nose. At –40°C, you can't stay outdoors for more than 10 minutes or your skin freezes. At –45°C, the metal on your glasses sticks to your face! I don't go out very much. People only walk short distances from one warm place to another. All activities happen indoors – from shopping to sports. A popular local sport that lots of boys do is wrestling. I don't wrestle. I like to jump rope, and I try to do it three or four times a week. Both jumping rope and wrestling use a lot of energy, and they keep you warm and strong. That's important when you live in subzero conditions!

In the summer, Yakutsk is a different city. In June and July, it's the season of "white nights," when the sky never gets dark, not even at midnight. The snow melts, and the temperature rises to 30°C and higher. Most people are happy to have a heat wave after 10 months of winter. Camping and barbecues are the favorite summer activities, with parties all night long. I'm thinking about summer weather a lot these days because there are still four more months of winter. I can't wait for summer!

DID YOU KNOW...?
The lowest ever recorded temperature in Yakutsk, Siberia, northeast Russia, was –64°C.

Reading: A blog

1. **Look at the title of the blog. What is special about the town of Yakutsk?**

2. **Read and listen to Meg's blog. Check your answer in Exercise 1.**

3. **Read the blog again. Answer the questions.**
   1. What are the average temperatures in Yakutsk in winter?
   _____
   2. What kinds of clothes do people wear outside in the winter?
   _____
   3. Why does it take a lot of time to get ready to go out in the winter?
   _____
   4. What is the season of "white nights"?
   _____
   5. What do people do in the summer in Yakutsk?
   _____

4. **YOUR TURN** **Work with a partner. Ask and answer the questions.**
   1. Would you like to live in Yakutsk? What are the good things about living there? What are the bad things?
   2. Are there any places in your country that are similar to Yakutsk?
   3. Which is the coldest region in your country? What's the hottest?
   4. How is life in your town different in summer and in winter? In what way?

   I wouldn't want to live in Yakutsk. It's too cold there!

Grammar: Simple present and present continuous review

5. Complete the chart.

Use the simple present to describe what normally happens. This includes routines and facts.	
The metal on your glasses **sticks** to your face.	I **don't like** hot weather.
I _____ cold weather. Winter **is** my favorite season.	We _____ **go out** a lot in the winter. It's too cold!
Use the present continuous to describe something happening right now or these days.	
I'm wearing a hat.	My friend **isn't studying** for tomorrow's test right now.
We're _____ a lot of hot food like soup these days because it's cold outside.	**I'm not** _____ boots because it's too hot outside for them.

▶ Check your answers: Grammar reference, p. 106

6. Circle the correct answers.

1. **I'm trying** / **I try** to stay inside the house these days.
2. When the weather is bad, most activities **happen** / **are happening** indoors.
3. My friends **love** / **are loving** cold weather.
4. **We watch** / **We're watching** the weather report on TV right now.
5. In my town, the snow **melts** / **is melting** only in April or May.
6. Matthew **plans** / **is planning** his vacation in the Bahamas right now.
7. My cousin moved to Costa Rica because she **doesn't like** / **isn't liking** cold winters.
8. Right now, Daniel and Elizabeth **put** / **are putting** their boots on to walk to school.

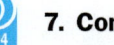

7. Complete the text with the simple present or present continuous forms of the verbs. Listen and check.

Mark and his family ¹_____*love*_____ (love) the place they live: Costa Rica. But this week, they ²_____ (live) a different life. They ³_____ (visit) their cousins in Barrow, Alaska. Costa Rica is a warm, tropical country. The temperature ⁴_____ (not change) much there. It's around 27°C all year round. The average temperature in Barrow is 11°C, and the temperature ⁵_____ (stay) below 0°C for 160 days of the year. Mark's in Barrow right now. He says, "I ⁶_____ (have) fun with my cousins this week, but we ⁷_____ (not go) outside much. I ⁸_____ (not have) the right clothes!" In Costa Rica, Mark usually ⁹_____ (play) soccer outside after school, but this week, he ¹⁰_____ (play) video games indoors. In Costa Rica, he ¹¹_____ (go) to the beach on Saturday or Sunday. In Barrow, he ¹²_____ (go) to hockey games. He says, "I can't wait to get back to hot weather!"

Speaking: It's too hot!

8. YOUR TURN Make notes about how hot weather and cold weather affect you. Then ask and answer the questions with a partner.

- What do you eat?
- How well do you sleep?
- Where do you exercise?
- What do you do for fun?

In really cold weather, I eat a lot of bread and soup. In really hot weather, I don't eat anything. I'm not hungry!

BE CURIOUS Find out about a family living in Alaska. What do they do in the winter when they don't have enough food? (Workbook, p. 72)

Discovery EDUCATION

1.1 THE LONG WINTER

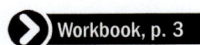

On the ROAD

Listening: Biking the Pan-American Highway

1. Look at the map of the Pan-American Highway. How many kilometers do you imagine the highway is? How long do you think it would take to travel the entire highway by bike?

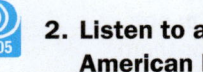

2. Listen to a radio program about a family's experience on the Pan-American Highway. How does Diane, the mother, feel now that the trip is finished?

3. Listen again. Circle the correct answers.

    1. How long is the Pan-American Highway?
        a. 28,000 kilometers   b. 100 kilometers   c. 13,000 kilometers
    2. In what country did the Miller family take a plane?
        a. Ecuador   b. Argentina   c. Panama
    3. How far did the family ride each day?
        a. between 11 and 13 kilometers   b. between 14 and 16 kilometers   c. between 50 and 100 kilometers
    4. How did the Miller family communicate with family members?
        a. They read blogs.   b. They wrote a blog post every week.
        c. They talked on the phone.
    5. What did Robert miss the most while he was traveling?
        a. having a home   b. free entertainment
        c. going to a different place every night
    6. How can listeners find out more about the Millers' trip?
        a. They can send an email to Robert and Diane.
        b. They can read the blog or Diane's book.
        c. They can read Diane's book or call her on the phone.

Vocabulary: Basic needs

4. Match the words and phrases with the words associated with them. Then listen and check your answers.

    1. ___ food and drink
    2. ___ clothes
    3. ___ entertainment
    4. ___ health care
    5. ___ transportation
    6. ___ communication
    7. ___ a home
    8. ___ education
    9. ___ money

    a. house, apartment
    b. movies, games, sports
    c. high school, college, homeschooling
    d. email, text messages, phone calls
    e. hospitals, laboratories, clinics
    f. spaghetti, salad, juice
    g. cash, credit cards, coins
    h. buses, trucks, bikes
    i. boots, jackets, hats

5. Look again at the words in Exercise 4. Write them in order of importance to you. Then discuss your list with your partner.

Grammar: Simple past and past continuous review

6. Complete the chart.

Use the simple past to describe actions and events in the past.	
We **took** a plane over part of Panama.	They **didn't have** to stop for food.
We _____ our own food.	He **didn't** _____ his arm, but it hurt a lot.
What _____ you **miss** the most?	
Use the past continuous to describe actions and events in progress in the past.	
I _____ **spending** the night in Quito when I heard that the road was closed.	He **wasn't wearing** a helmet when he fell.
They _____ **eating** their lunch by the road when the storm started.	You **weren't talking** to me when I dropped my phone.
What **were** you _____ last night when the electricity went out?	

> Check your answers: Grammar reference, p. 106

7. Circle the correct answers.

1. My bike **broke** / **was breaking** down while I **rode** / **was riding** through Mexico.
2. When she **studied** / **was studying** in Greece, Evelyn **bought** / **was buying** food from local markets.
3. I **sat** / **was sitting** in the park when I **heard** / **was hearing** the news.
4. When the hail **began** / **was beginning**, I **talked** / **was talking** on the phone.
5. You **called** / **were calling** while I **watched** / **was watching** the football game.
6. Neil and Austin **drove** / **were driving** through the blizzard when they **ran** / **were running** out of gas.

8. Complete the sentences with the correct form of *used to* and the verbs in parentheses.

1. I _____ (think) everyone in South America spoke Spanish, but now I know that people in Brazil speak Portuguese.
2. Steve _____ (not ride) his bike much, but now he rides it every day.
3. My grandparents _____ (not come) to see us often, but now they visit every month.
4. Public transportation _____ (be) terrible in this town, but now we have a great subway system.
5. We _____ (not cook) a lot of meals at home, but now we only go to restaurants on special occasions.

used to

Use used to *when something happened over a period of time but doesn't happen anymore.*

I **used to be** a swimmer, but now I play soccer.

We **didn't use to ride** our bikes a lot, but now we ride every day.

Did you **use to live** in Boston?

Speaking: Last night and long ago

9. YOUR TURN Use the phrases below to write five questions. You can use the simple past or past continuous.

what	do	last night
when	go	when you were younger
where	eat	
	live	

10. Work in pairs. Ask and answer your questions.

> What were you doing last night?

> I was doing my homework. What about you?

 Say it **RIGHT!**

In statements, *used to* often sounds like /justə/. Listen and repeat the sentences.

I **used to** spend a lot of money on public transportation, but now I ride my bike.

He **used to** like living in Canada, but he doesn't anymore. It's too cold!

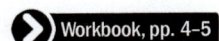

REAL TALK | 1.2 WHICH DO YOU PREFER – TOWNS AND CITIES OR THE COUNTRY?

A Great Place TO LIVE

Conversation: City, town, or country?

1. **REAL TALK** Watch or listen to the teenagers. Check (✓) the things that the teenagers like about living in the city.

   ☐ bike riding ☐ fresh air ☐ looking at animals
   ☐ concerts ☐ hiking ☐ different neighborhoods
   ☐ shopping ☐ museums ☐ parks

2. **YOUR TURN** Which do you prefer – small towns, cities, or the country? Tell your partner.

3. Listen to Kate talking to Mark about Greenville. Complete the conversation.

   USEFUL LANGUAGE: Agreeing and disagreeing
   don't you think? | ✓Don't you agree? | I don't think so. | See what I mean? | I disagree.

   Kate: Do you live near school, Mark?
   Mark: No, I live in Greenville. Have you been there?
   Kate: Yes, I live there, too. It's a great place to live. ¹ *Don't you agree?*
   Mark: Well, it's really quiet. Actually, nothing ever happens, and there's nothing to do. It's boring.
   Kate: Well, ² _____ There are lots of things to do. What about the new mall and the community center?
   Mark: Maybe, but all my friends live here, in the city, and I can't go out with them in the evening.
   Kate: Yeah, but Greenville is healthier, ³ _____
   Mark: The air, you mean? ⁴ _____ It's close to the city, so I don't think living in Greenville makes a difference. And there's so much heavy rain.
   Kate: Well, if there's heavy rain in Greenville, there's heavy rain in the city, too. They both have the same weather.
   Mark: That's true. I like taking my dog for walks. Greenville is good for that.
   Kate: ⁵ _____ It's not all bad.
   Mark: That's true. Maybe you're right. Small towns are OK, but I still wish I lived in the city.

4. Practice the conversation with a partner.

5. **YOUR TURN** Work with a partner. Take turns giving your opinion. Then agree and disagree.

Situation 1	Situation 2
Living in a city.	Going to a big school.
Good: lots to do, easy to travel around	Good: lots of facilities, clubs, variety of different subjects to study
Bad: noisy, stressful, unhealthy	Bad: noisy, impersonal, more bullying

   There's a lot to do in the city, and that's good, don't you think?

   Well, I like small towns. They're not as noisy as big cities. . . .

To: laura@net.cup.org
From: addison@net.cup.org
Subject: A fun vacation

Hi Laura!

I'd like you to come visit me this summer. I miss you! You live in a big city, but I live in a cabin by a lake and that's cool, too. Ask your parents if you can spend a week with me and my family this summer. Here's what you can tell them:

First of all, we can do lots of fun stuff. For example, we can go swimming all day, every day. My family also has a boat, and we can go water skiing or visit other places on the lake. There's an island in the middle of the lake, and we can have a barbecue there.

Second, it's healthy to be out here by the lake. You'll get a lot of exercise. For instance, we can go hiking in the woods (and we can go swimming again when we come back!). We can shop for organic food at the farmers' market. And there's no pollution, and this part of the state is really clean and nice.

The best part is that we can be together! I haven't seen you in six months. That's a long time.

I really hope you can visit us this summer! Talk to your mom and dad. If they have any questions, they can talk to my parents.

Love,
Addison

Reading to write: A persuasive email

6. Look at the pictures and read Addison's email to Laura. What does she want Laura to do?

> ● *Focus on* **CONTENT**
> When you write a persuasive email, you can follow this format:
> - Start with a topic sentence that states your position on something.
> - Explain why you think your readers should do what you're suggesting. Start your sentences with phrases such as *First of all*, *Second*, and *The best part*.
> - Close your email by stating your position again. Try to say it in a different way this time.

7. Find examples of each of the points in Focus on Content in Addison's email.

> ● *Focus on* **LANGUAGE**
> **Introducing details**
> *For example* and *for instance* are similar in meaning.
> - There's a lot to do in the city. **For Instance** / **For example**, you can visit art museums.

Writing: A persuasive email

◯ **PLAN**
Think of something you'd like to persuade someone else to do. Use the list in the Focus on Content box and make notes.

◯ **WRITE**
Write your email. Use your notes from above to help you. Write about 150 words.

◯ **CHECK**
Check your writing. Can you say "yes" to these questions?

- Have you followed the instructions in the Focus on Content box?
- Did you use *for example* or *for instance*?

8. Match the sentences.

1. There are lots of fun things to do in the mountains. For example, ___
2. We have lots of different kinds of weather here. For instance, ___
3. There are lots of great restaurants in my town. For instance, ___
4. Mary eats an unhealthy amount of sugar every day. For example, ___

a. today she had doughnuts and soda for breakfast, an ice-cream sundae for dessert at lunch, and a big piece of cake at dinner.

b. we have Greek ones, Italian ones, and my favorite, a place that only serves pancakes.

c. you can ride horses, hike, or go camping.

d. we have blizzards in the winter, heavy rains in the spring, and heat waves in the summer.

Tristan da Cunha

The most remote inhabited island on Earth!

Tristan da Cunha, the most remote inhabited island on the planet, is in the middle of the Atlantic Ocean. It's over 2,800 kilometers from the nearest land, and to get there, you need to fly to Cape Town, in South Africa. Then, because there's no airport on the island, you have to travel by ship for seven days.

Tristan da Cunha was named after the Portuguese discoverer who first saw the island. Although it is almost 10,000 kilometers from London, it's part of a British territory. The official language is English, but the people who live there also speak a local dialect. The British monarch is the head of state, and they use British pounds as their currency.

The island is very small – only 11 kilometers long. Queen Mary Peak, a volcano in the middle of the island, is 2,000 meters high, and it's active, too! The weather doesn't get too hot or too cold, but there are times of heavy rain.

The island is home to 80 families, about 260 people in total, and they have only eight last names. These are the last names of some of the first people to settle on the island. There is only one town and one school, and that's the only place with an Internet connection.

In October 1961, the island's volcano erupted, and the whole population went to live in the UK. They got jobs and new homes, but they didn't like living so far from their island. They weren't used to the noise, the traffic, and the cold winter. So, in November 1962, 200 islanders returned to Tristan da Cunha and their old lives there. They were happier without television, cars, and the stress of modern life!

DID YOU KNOW...?

Many of the original settlers of the island had asthma. Over 50 percent of the people on Tristan da Cunha have asthma now. Scientists have learned a lot about the disease by studying the people of the island.

Culture: A remote island

1. Look at the picture. Where do you think this place is? What is special about it?

2. Read and listen to the article. Check your answers in Exercise 1.

3. Read the article again. Complete the table.

Approximate distance from the nearest land:	2,800 kilometers
Official language:	
Approximate distance from London:	
Length of island:	
Number of families:	
Number of schools:	
Month and year that the volcano erupted:	
Number of people who returned to Tristan da Cunha in 1962:	

4. **YOUR TURN** Work with a partner. Ask and answer the questions.
   1. Would you like to visit Tristan da Cunha? Why? / Why not?
   2. What do you think are the good things about living on the island? What are the bad things?

BE CURIOUS Find out about the people in Bali, India. What are their two main foods? (Workbook, p. 73)

1.3 AN ISLAND FLOOD

UNIT 1 REVIEW

Vocabulary

1. Write the extreme weather word for each picture.

1. _fog_   2. _____

3. _____   4. _____

5. _____   6. _____

Grammar

2. Complete the sentences.

1. You can't go outside right now. It _'s raining_ (rain) really hard!
2. I _____ (work) after school and on the weekends to make extra money.
3. My teacher _____ (not talk) right now. She's writing a report at her desk.
4. We _____ (not like) cold weather. That's why we live in Florida.
5. My little brother _____ (cry) when there is thunder and lightning.
6. The chef is in the restaurant kitchen. He _____ (make) a special soup.

3. Circle the correct answers.

1. The surfer **swam** / **was swimming** in the ocean when she saw the shark.
2. When I was younger, I **watched** / **used to watch** a lot of TV. I don't anymore.
3. It **rained** / **used to rain** about 10 centimeters last night.
4. What **did you do** / **were you doing** at 9:00 p.m. last night?
5. My sister **wasn't thinking** / **didn't use to think** that education was important. Now she studies really hard.
6. I **did** / **was doing** all my homework. Do you want to play a video game?

Useful language

4. Complete the conversation.

you agree	think
See what I	disagree

John: Hey, Dylan. My family is taking a vacation abroad this summer. We might go to Canada.

Dylan: Canada? There are blizzards there! The weather is pretty harsh, don't you ¹_____?

John: Actually, it's nice in the summer. What about you? What are your plans?

Dylan: I want to learn Spanish. My friend Mike is visiting his grandma in Colombia, and he invited me to come. I can learn a lot of Spanish. Don't ²_____?

John: No. Mike's American. You won't learn Spanish.

Dylan: I ³_____. I can learn from his grandma!

John: Well, maybe you're right. It'll be fun, even if you don't learn a lot of Spanish.

Dylan: ⁴_____ mean? It's a great idea!

PROGRESS CHECK: Now I can . . .

- ☐ talk about extreme weather.
- ☐ discuss how my environment affects my life.
- ☐ talk about past incidents and habits.
- ☐ ask for agreement.
- ☐ write a persuasive email.
- ☐ discuss a faraway place.

CLIL PROJECT

1.4 LIFE IN THE DESERT, p. 116

2 First Things FIRST!

Discovery EDUCATION

BE CURIOUS

- Get Up and Go!
- What do you think makes a good friend?
- Irish Dancing

1. What do you see in this photo?

2. How busy are you? Do you have lots of different things going on in your life?

3. How do you feel about all your different activities?

UNIT CONTENTS

Vocabulary Priorities; emotions
Grammar have to/don't have to; must; Modals of obligation – should, ought to, had better; It's + adjective + infinitive
Listening Take it easy!

Vocabulary: Priorities

1. Match the photos (a–h) with the phrases.

1. _b_ shopping for clothes
2. ___ working out
3. ___ hanging out with friends
4. ___ doing something creative
5. ___ getting enough sleep
6. ___ having time for yourself
7. ___ helping around the house
8. ___ chatting with friends online
9. ___ staying out late on the weekend

2. Listen, check, and repeat.

3. What activities are the words below associated with? Write phrases from Exercise 1 in the correct place below.

1. making a cake or writing a song _____
2. going to parties or movies at night _____
3. lifting weights or doing exercises _____
4. washing the dishes, cleaning your room _____
5. taking a walk, reading a book _____
6. watching TV, playing games, talking _____

Speaking: What matters most?

4. YOUR TURN Work with a partner. Ask and answer the questions.

1. Which thing in the list in Exercise 1 is most important to you? Why?
2. Which things do you argue about with your parents?
3. Which thing stresses you the most? Why?

> Let's see. I think the most important thing for me is having time for myself – so I can just relax and do what I want to do!

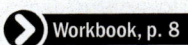
Workbook, p. 8

Reading Getting Some Shut-Eye; Stories of Stress; Ten Things I Bet You Didn't Know About . . . Cheerleading
Conversation Helping someone to do something
Writing A blog post about solving a problem

Unit 2 | 13

Time for BED

Getting Some Shut-Eye

Did You Know?
Teenagers who sleep enough:
> usually have better skin than those who don't sleep enough.
> eat less junk food than teens who don't.
> are less likely to experience depression than those who don't.

Teenagers have to get more sleep! According to researchers, teenagers need to sleep a lot more than adults: eight to 10 hours every night. Sadly, only 15 percent of teenagers sleep eight hours on a school night, and that's just not enough.

Here are three reasons to get more sleep:

Your body needs sleep.
Your body is still growing, and your brain is still developing. Teenagers shouldn't forget how much their bodies need that extra sleep.

Sleep helps you do better in school.
When you're tired, you can't concentrate very well. And when you can't concentrate, it's difficult to learn.

Sleep keeps you healthy.
Without enough sleep, your body gets weak, and it's easy for you to catch colds and other illnesses. Tired people often eat food with more sugar in it, and that isn't good for you.

What can you do to get more sleep?
> Don't drink anything with caffeine at night, including soda.
> If you're hungry, have a light snack. That sometimes helps people sleep.
> One hour before you go to bed, turn off the TV and shut down your computer.
> Don't take your cell phone to bed with you!

Reading: A magazine article

1. **Look at the picture. How many hours of sleep do you think teenagers need?**

2. **Read and listen to the article about teenagers and sleep. What's the main aim of the article?**
   a. to tell parents what to do about teenagers who sleep a lot
   b. to offer advice to teenagers about how to get up earlier in the morning
   c. to tell teenagers why sleep is important and how to get more of it

3. **Read the article again and answer the questions.**
   1. What is one reason teenagers may feel depressed or sad?
   2. How many hours of sleep do most teenagers need?
   3. What percentage of teenagers sleep eight hours on school nights?
   4. What can happen at school if you don't get enough sleep?
   5. What kind of food do tired people usually eat more of?
   6. What should you do one hour before you go to bed?

4. **YOUR TURN** Work with a partner. Ask and answer the questions.
   1. What time do you usually go to bed during the week? Do you find it difficult to get to sleep? Why? / Why not?
   2. Do you think you get enough sleep? What kinds of things keep you from getting a good night's sleep? What happens if you don't sleep enough?

> *What time do you usually go to bed during the week?*

> *I usually go to bed around 11:00. What about you?*

Say it RIGHT!

Notice the different sounds of the letter c. Can you find another example of each in the article?

/s/	/k/
ne**ce**ssary	**ca**ffeine

Grammar: *have to/don't have to*

5. Complete the chart.

Use have/has to *to say that it is necessary to do something.*
Use don't/doesn't have to *to say that it is not necessary to do something, but you can do it if you want to.*

Affirmative	Negative
I _____ **get** more sleep.	I _____ **get up** early on Saturdays.
My brother _____ **get up** early on Saturdays. He works in a restaurant.	My little sister _____ **help** with the housework. She's only two.

> Check your answers: Grammar reference, p. 107

6. Complete the sentences with the correct form of *have to*.

1. A professional tennis player _____ train for four or five hours every day.
2. I _____ study math three or four hours every night. It's really difficult for me!
3. My mom is a piano teacher, so I _____ pay for my piano lessons.
4. My brother is really lucky. He _____ do any homework. He's only three years old.
5. My parents _____ work on weekends, so we usually do something fun together.
6. My best friend _____ get up early on Saturday. His baseball practice starts at 8:00 a.m.

7. Use the words to write sentences. Use *must* or *must not*.

1. You / eat in the classroom
   _____
2. You / wear your seat belt in the car
   _____
3. You / leave trash on the beach
   _____
4. You / come to school on time
   _____
5. You / clean up your trash when you go camping
   _____
6. You / take scissors on a plane
   _____

must

Use must/must not *to talk about rules, laws, or prohibited actions.*

You **must** be quiet in the library.	You **must not** touch the art in a museum.
She **must** return her books on time.	He **must not** use his cell phone here.

Speaking: *Do you have to . . . ?*

8. YOUR TURN Work with a partner. Ask and answer questions using *Do you have to . . .* and the phrases.

clean your room	practice a musical instrument
get up early on Saturday or Sunday	study English over the weekend
go to bed at a specific time	take care of your younger brother or sister
help cook meals	wash the dishes

> Do you have to take care of your younger sister?

> Yes, sometimes I do, when my parents have to work late.

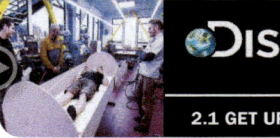

BE CURIOUS — Find out about a new way to wake up in the morning. Do you think the machine is a good idea? (Workbook, p. 74)

2.1 GET UP AND GO!

Stressed OUT!

Listening: Take it easy!

1. Look at the girl in the picture above. How does she feel? What are some reasons she might feel that way?

2. Listen to a radio interview with a psychologist, Dr. Hilary Jamieson, talking about teenage stress. What are the three essential tips Dr. Jamieson gives?

3. Listen again. Circle the things Dr. Jamieson suggests.
   1. Make a schedule and keep to it.
   2. Go out with your friends and have a good time.
   3. Participate in a sport.
   4. Listen to music or watch TV.
   5. Talk to someone.
   6. Breathe deeply and try to relax.

Vocabulary: Emotions

4. Match the words with the correct pictures. Then listen and check your answers.
   1. ___ embarrassed
   2. ___ awful
   3. ___ proud
   4. ___ terrified
   5. ___ stressed out
   6. ___ exhausted
   7. ___ wonderful

5. Think of a time when you or someone you know felt one of the emotions in Exercise 4. Tell your partner about it.

> I felt stressed out last week. I had a lot of homework, and my mother was mad at me, too.

> Really? I felt wonderful last week. This week I feel exhausted because . . .

Grammar: Modals of obligation – *should, ought to, had better*

6. Complete the chart.

Should, ought to, and had better have similar meanings. Use them to say what is a good or right thing to do.		
Use *should* and *shouldn't* for a personal opinion.	Use *ought to* and *ought not to* when you're talking about duty or the law.	Use *had better* and *had better not* to give very strong advice.
You **should try** to work out more.	I _____ **call** the police about the car accident.	You **had better start** studying for your test now.
He _____ **get** so stressed out.	You **ought not to enter** that part of the airport.	You _____ **be** late for the test.

> Check your answers: Grammar reference, p. 107

7. Choose the correct answers.

1. If you're sick, you **had better / had better not** see a doctor.
2. My brother doesn't know what he **should / shouldn't** do about college.
3. You **ought / ought not** to park your car here. It's illegal.
4. We **should / shouldn't** go see a movie when we have so much work to do.
5. She **ought / ought not** to be more careful when she's cooking. She always burns herself.
6. I **had better / had better not** bother my father right now. He's really busy.

8. Use the words in parentheses to write + (affirmative) or − (negative) sentences.

1. It's <u>not easy to find</u> enough time to study sometimes. (− / easy / to find)
2. It's _____ some exercise every day. (+ / important / to get)
3. It's _____ with friends on the weekend. (+ / relaxing / to hang out)
4. It's _____ too many after-school activities. (− / smart / to do)
5. It's _____ all your time studying. (− / fun / to spend)
6. It's _____ your arms and legs when you're taking a test. (+ / helpful / to stretch)

> **It's + adjective + infinitive**
> Use It's + adjective + infinitive to give your opinion.
> **It's important to talk** to others when you're stressed.
> **It's not helpful to think** negative thoughts.

> **Get it RIGHT!**
> Use *to* after *ought*.
> You **ought to call** the police.
>
> Don't use *to* after *should* or *had better*.
> You **should drink** less coffee.
> You **had better leave** for school now.

Speaking: Do I have to?

9. Read the situations below. Check (✓) the ones you have experienced.

- ☐ I'm really tired, but I have so much homework to do!
- ☐ I really want to get on the school team this year, but I need to practice hard!
- ☐ My parents got mad at me last night because I came home really late.
- ☐ I argued with my best friend, and now he/she won't respond to my texts.

10. YOUR TURN Work with a partner. Take turns reading each of the situations in Exercise 9 and giving advice.

> My parents got mad at me last night because I came home really late.

> You should call them next time and tell them where you are.

 REAL TALK 2.2 WHAT DO YOU THINK MAKES A GOOD FRIEND?

Best Friends
FOREVER

Conversation: What makes a good friend?

 1. **REAL TALK** Watch or listen to the teenagers. Check (✓) the things they say.

- ☐ buys good birthday presents
- ☐ does all the same activities
- ☐ just has to be there
- ☐ is kind and helpful
- ☐ helps with decisions
- ☐ helps with homework
- ☐ likes to go out on the weekend
- ☐ likes to talk on the phone
- ☐ listens
- ☐ is honest

2. What do you think makes a good friend? What would you add to the list above?

 3. Listen to Olivia ask Laura about a school project. Complete the conversation.

USEFUL LANGUAGE: Helping someone to do something

- I'm not very good at things like that.
- It's really pretty simple.
- ✓ I'm not sure how to do it.
- Let me show you.
- I'll give you a hand if you like.

Olivia: Hey, Laura. Can I ask you something?
Laura: Yeah, sure. What's up?
Olivia: It's this science project. [1] _I'm not sure how to do it._
Laura: Mr. Brown's really strict about it. He put instructions on the school intranet.
Olivia: Oh! I should look, then. Do you know how to get access to the intranet?
Laura: Yes, you have to type in your password.
[2] _____ See? Type it like this, and click "Submit."
Olivia: Thanks. That's really nice of you!
Laura: [3] _____ You shouldn't have any problems with it. Just make sure you format it correctly.
Olivia: Oh, no! [4] _____
Laura: Don't worry. [5] _____
Olivia: Great! Thanks a lot.

4. Practice the conversation with a partner.

5. **YOUR TURN** Work with a partner. Take turns asking for and giving help. Use the following ideas or your own ideas.

Situation 1: You want to download a video, but you don't know how.
Possible steps: Find the video; click on the "Download" button; name the video and click "Save."

Situation 2: You can't find any material for a school project.
Possible steps: Find online sources; go to the library; find people to interview.

Stories of STRESS

STUDYING HARD?
STRESSED OUT?
TOO MUCH TO DO?

Tell us your story. What was the problem and how did you feel? How did you solve it and what's your advice to students with similar problems? We publish the best stories on our website!

MIKE, SAN DIEGO, CA: I have a story to tell about a time last month when I had too much to do. And I think I have some great advice. The problem was that I had a big history test and besides that, I had a lot of other projects to do, too. I was super stressed out. I was studying hard one Saturday afternoon, for about three hours straight. Then a friend came over. He helped me solve the problem. He said, "Take a little time off!" We had a snack, and then we took my dog for a walk. Then I started studying again. What happened? I was relaxed, I had more energy, and I was able to study for the rest of the day. Best of all, I got an A on the test! My advice: You have to take a break sometimes.

Reading to write: Solving a problem

○ *Focus on* **CONTENT**

When you're writing about a solution to a problem, it's necessary to tell the reader what the problem is. Then tell the reader your solution to the problem in clear steps. You can write these steps in order of their importance. Start with the most important step.

6. Read Mike's blog post. Answer the questions.

1. What was the problem?
2. How did Mike feel?
3. How did he solve it?
4. What is Mike's advice to other students?

○ *Focus on* **LANGUAGE**
Quantifiers: *a few, a little, too many, too much*

- Use *a few* and *a little* to talk about a small amount or number. Use *a few* with plural countable nouns, and *a little* with uncountable nouns.
  - *We played a video game for **a few** minutes.*
  - *I decided to take **a little** time off.*
- Use *too many* and *too much* to talk about things that are "more than is good for the situation."
  - *I had **too many** other projects to do.*
  - *He said I was studying **too much**.*

Writing: A blog post

◯ **PLAN**

Think about a time you were stressed out or had too much to do. What was the problem? How did you feel and how did you solve it? What's your advice to other students who have the same problem?

◯ **WRITE**

Write your blog post. Use your notes from Exercise 6 and Mike's story to help you. Write 80–100 words.

◯ **CHECK**

Check your writing. Can you answer "yes" to these questions?

- Did you say what the problem is?
- Did you give a solution in clear steps?
- Did you state the steps to the solution in order of importance?

7. Complete the sentences with *a few, a little, too many,* and *too much*.

1. David only has _____ books in his backpack. It isn't heavy.
2. I brought _____ food for lunch today. Would you like half of this sandwich?
3. There were _____ people in line for the movie, so we left without seeing it.
4. I can go to bed early because I only have _____ homework today.

Ten Things I Bet You Didn't Know About... CHEERLEADING

1. Cheerleading is more than 100 years old! The first cheerleading team came out to support the University of Minnesota football team in November 1889.

2. Today, more than 97 percent of all cheerleaders are female, but 100 years ago they were all male.

3. Now, on college or university cheerleading squads in the United States, half of the members are male.

4. Cheerleading is very competitive, and it's difficult to make most squads. The successful candidates often have to spend their summers training together for the next season.

5. Football is the main sport associated with cheerleading, but there are also cheerleaders for basketball, soccer, baseball, and even wrestling!

6. Cheerleading is a great way to fight stress. It also helps you feel good and make friends!

7. Cheerleading won't hurt your grades! It's important to have discipline – as an athlete and as a student. Cheerleading helps with this.

8. Cheerleading is hard physical work. Cheerleaders train hard – as hard as the football players they support – and they have to be very fit. Ninety-eight percent of female cheerleaders are also gymnasts.

9. Cheerleading can be dangerous. Many cheerleaders injure their arms and legs. Some also injure their backs and heads.

10. Cheerleading started in the United States and is still very much an American activity, but there are organized cheerleaders in more than 31 countries around the world.

Culture: Cheerleading

1. **Look at the photos and answer the questions.**
   1. Where are the people? What are they doing?
   2. What do you know about cheerleading? Make a list.

2. **Read and listen to the article. Does it mention any of the facts you wrote in Exercise 1?**

3. **Read the article again. Are the sentences below true (*T*) or false (*F*)?**
   1. All cheerleaders are girls. ___
   2. Cheerleaders only support football teams. ___
   3. Most cheerleaders don't do well in school. ___
   4. Cheerleading is hard work. ___
   5. Cheerleading is a very safe activity. ___
   6. Cheerleaders only exist in the United States. ___

4. **YOUR TURN** **Work with a partner. Ask and answer the questions.**
   1. Would you like to be a cheerleader? Why? / Why not?
   2. Why do you think cheerleading helps students' grades?
   3. What are the most popular school sports and activities in your country? Do you think these sports can help you do better in school? Why? / Why not?

DID YOU KNOW...?
There are more than 4 million cheerleaders in the world.

 Find out about an Irish dance champion. How is Irish dance different from dance in your country? (Workbook, p. 75)

2.3 IRISH DANCING

UNIT 2 REVIEW

Vocabulary

1. Complete the sentences.

| get enough sleep | do something creative |
| time for myself | help around the house |

1. I need to be alone sometimes. I need _____.
2. My mom sometimes asks me to _____. I hate cleaning the bathroom!
3. I'm always tired because I don't _____.
4. I want to be a designer or an artist because I want to _____.

2. Match the sentences.

1. I just fell down in the hall outside of class. ___
2. I just ran five kilometers! ___
3. I have four big tests this week. ___
4. My sister's volleyball team just won a big game. ___

a. I'm proud of them.
b. I'm really stressed out.
c. I'm exhausted.
d. I'm so embarrassed!

Grammar

3. Write sentences with *should* (✓) or *shouldn't* (✗).

1. You / play computer games in the evening (✗)
   You shouldn't play computer games in the evening.
2. Teenagers / help their families on the weekends (✓)
   _____
3. You / use your cell phone before bed (✗)
   _____
4. My sister is stressed out. She / talk to a friend (✓)
   _____
5. Teenagers / eat healthy food whenever they can (✓)
   _____
6. I / watch TV right now (✗)
   _____

4. Fill in the blanks with the correct form of *have to*.

1. You ___*have to*___ be quiet in the library.
2. The basketball game is free. We _____ pay for tickets.
3. Julio wears jeans and T-shirts to school. He _____ wear a uniform.
4. Students _____ eat in the cafeteria. They are allowed to leave the school for lunch.
5. Mike _____ study for his math test tonight. He can't go out.

Useful language

5. Complete the conversation.

| Let me show you. | I'm not very good at things like that. | I'm not sure how to do it. |

Kate: Oh, no.
Pete: Are you OK? What do you need?
Kate: I'm just stressed out about my science homework. ¹_____ I need some coffee, I think.
Pete: Don't drink coffee now. Make some herbal tea.
Kate: Make herbal tea? ²_____
Pete: Look. ³_____ It's easy.
Kate: It is?
Pete: Yes. Boil some water and pour it over a tea bag. Like this.
Kate: That *was* easy. Hey, this tea is good!

PROGRESS CHECK: Now I can . . .

☐ discuss my priorities.
☐ express obligation and prohibition.
☐ write a blog post to help someone solve a problem.
☐ make strong recommendations.
☐ offer help to someone.
☐ discuss a sport or cultural activity.

3 ART All Around Us

Discovery EDUCATION
BE CURIOUS

- Original Art
- Have you ever been to a concert?
- A World of Music
- Art in Perspective

1. Describe what you see in this picture.
2. What is your opinion of this kind of art?
3. In what ways is this kind of art different from art you see in museums?

UNIT CONTENTS

Vocabulary Visual arts; musical instruments
Grammar Verb + -ing form (gerund) review; -ing forms (gerunds) as subjects; verbs + prepositions + -ing forms
Listening Leo the one-man band

Vocabulary: Visual arts

1. Match the people, places, and things with the correct pictures.

1. _g_ comics
2. ___ living statue
3. ___ digital art
4. ___ sculpture
5. ___ drawing
6. ___ mural
7. ___ exhibition
8. ___ pottery
9. ___ graffiti
10. ___ portrait painter

2. Listen, check, and repeat.

3. Put the words from Exercise 1 in the correct categories.
   a. Works of art: _____
   b. Place to see art: _____
   c. A performer or an artist: _____

Speaking: Look again

4. **YOUR TURN** Put the words from Exercise 1 in new categories.

Cool	Educational	Strange

5. Work with a partner. Share your opinions about kinds of art.

   I like looking at comics. They're really cool.

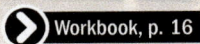
Workbook, p. 16

Reading Everyone's an Artist; Fantastic Free Concert; A Temporary Desert City
Conversation Inviting a friend and arranging to meet
Writing A blog post about a concert

Unit 3 | 23

WHAT is ART?

EVERYONE'S AN ARTIST

You draw, you paint portraits, you do sculptures, or you're a living statue. It doesn't matter — everyone's an artist!

THE CASE FOR We look at the *Mona Lisa* or a Picasso painting, and we say, "That's art." But what about the amazing graffiti on your street? What about photographs posted online by our friends? What about your school art exhibition? You worked hard, and it's great. So, is that art? To me, art is anything that's creative. Of course, I like going to famous museums. But I also like drawing portraits of my friends. I'm not very good, but I'm creative. I'm passionate about it, and my friends like it. Most of all, I like it!
Josh, age 15, San Diego, California

THE CASE AGAINST I like visiting art museums, too. Why? Because I like looking at good art. Art is not the drawings of four-year-old children. It isn't painting your body crazy colors and standing in the street. And it certainly isn't graffiti. Some people say, "If it's creative and cool, it's art." I don't agree. Art is the result of hard work and study. My aunt is an artist. She went to art school for six years. She doesn't make much money, but sometimes her sculptures are in exhibitions. Her art is great. Art is very hard, and not many people can do it well.
Kayla, age 16, Charlotte, North Carolina

WHAT IS ART? WHAT'S YOUR OPINION?

DID YOU KNOW...?
The British graffiti artist Banksy sold a piece of graffiti for $1.8 million.

Reading: An online debate

1. **Work with a partner. Ask and answer the questions.**
    1. Do you ever see art that you think is terrible? Why do you think it's bad?
    2. What makes a person an artist?
    3. Do you have friends or family members who are artists?

2. **Read and listen to the debate. How do Josh and Kayla define "art"?**

3. **Read the debate again. Are the statements true (*T*) or false (*F*)?**
    1. Josh thinks that graffiti is art. ___
    2. Kayla enjoys going to art museums. ___
    3. To Josh, photographs posted online aren't examples of art. ___
    4. Kayla believes that art is anything that is creative and fun. ___
    5. Josh and his friends like the portraits he draws. ___
    6. Kayla thinks that good art is easy. ___

4. **YOUR TURN Work with a partner. Ask and answer the questions.**
    1. What's your opinion in the art debate? Is everyone an artist?
    2. What kind of background or education do you think an artist should have?
    3. Is graffiti art? If so, is all graffiti art or only some graffiti?
    4. Are pictures you take with your cell phone and then post online art? Why or why not?

> I think graffiti is sometimes good art. There's an artist in my neighborhood who . . .

Grammar: Verb + -ing form (gerund) review

5. Complete the chart.

We can use the -ing form of a verb after some verbs to talk about things we like or don't like.

Common verbs followed by -ing forms:
like, love, hate, enjoy, (not) mind

	-ing form	
I **love**	_drawing_ (draw)	pictures in my free time.
Mark **enjoys**	_____ (look)	at sculptures.
My sister **hates**	_____ (help)	around the house.
Some people **don't like**	_____ (go)	to museums.

> Check your answers: Grammar reference, p. 108

Get it RIGHT!
Use the -ing form after *enjoy*.
I **enjoy going** to art exhibitions. NOT: I enjoy to go to art exhibitions.

Say it RIGHT!
When you like or don't like something strongly, use *love* or *hate* and put extra stress on that verb. Listen and repeat the sentences.
I **love** painting. I **hate** shopping.

6. Complete the sentences with the correct forms of the verbs.

1. My friends ____love going____ (love / go) to the movies on the weekends.
2. I _____ (not mind / spend) time at art exhibits, but not more than two hours at a time.
3. Oscar _____ (enjoy / paint) murals, but not portraits.
4. My father _____ (not like / shop) for clothes. He never goes to the mall.
5. Some of my friends _____ (hate / read) comics, but I enjoy it a lot.
6. I _____ (like / study) in the library, not alone at home.

7. Circle the correct answers. Then complete the sentences.

| get up | ✓ live | paint | take |
| go | meet | sleep | work out |

My name is Jill, and I'm a professional artist. I live in Los Angeles. I ¹**like / don't like** ____living____ here because Los Angeles is full of open-minded, creative people. Mornings are my favorite time of the day, and I ²**love / hate** _____ early. Because it's sunny but not hot outside, I really ³**hate / like** _____ a long walk before I start work. It's great exercise. I usually paint for a few hours, maybe from 9:00 to 12:00, and then I have lunch. I ⁴**don't enjoy / enjoy** _____ friends for lunch. We usually make lunch together. After lunch, I ⁵**like / don't mind** _____ for about 30 minutes. Then I go back to work. I ⁶**finish / keep** _____ in the evening, about 7:00 or 8:00 p.m. I ⁷**love / don't love** _____ at the gym or going running on the beach. And, I ⁸**like / hate** _____ to bed late. I'm usually asleep by 9:00 or 10:00. It's a busy life, but I'm happy.

Speaking: I love shopping!

8. YOUR TURN Work with a partner. Tell your partner about the things you like and don't like doing.

Like	Don't like
don't mind, enjoy, like, love	don't enjoy, don't like, hate

> I like staying up late at night. I don't enjoy getting up early!

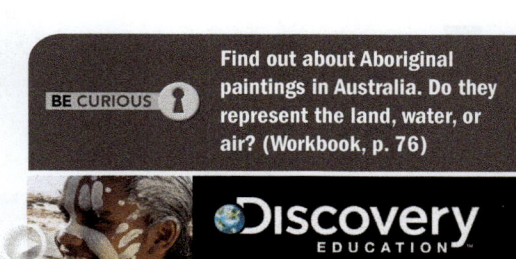

BE CURIOUS Find out about Aboriginal paintings in Australia. Do they represent the land, water, or air? (Workbook, p. 76)

3.1 ORIGINAL ART

> Workbook, pp. 16–17

MUSIC Everywhere!

Listening: Leo the one-man band

1. What do you imagine a one-man band is? Where do you think he performs?

2. Listen to Marcia, a journalist, interviewing Leo. Check your answers in Exercise 1.

3. Listen again. Answer the questions.
   1. Where are Marcia and Leo?
   2. Where are two places that Leo plays music?
   3. Which of Leo's instruments is new?
   4. How long did Leo play on the day of the interview?
   5. What types of music does he like playing?
   6. Which instruments does he not know how to play?

Vocabulary: Musical instruments

4. Match the words with the correct pictures. Then listen and check your answers.

   1. ___ guitar
   2. ___ drums
   3. ___ flute
   4. ___ saxophone
   5. ___ violin
   6. ___ keyboard
   7. ___ harmonica
   8. ___ piano
   9. ___ trumpet
   10. ___ cello

5. **YOUR TURN** Work with a partner. Ask and answer the questions.
   1. What instruments can you play? How long did it take to learn to play them?
   2. What kind of music do you enjoy listening to?
   3. Where can you go in your town to listen to musicians playing in the street?

26 | Unit 3

Grammar: -ing forms (gerunds) as subjects

6. Complete the chart.

> You can use the -ing form as the subject of a sentence.
> ___Playing___ (play) several instruments at once takes a lot of energy.
> _____ (sing) at the same time I play instruments is hard.
> _____ (be) here at the festival is really special to me.
>
> For the negative, use not before the -ing form.
>
> **Not enjoying** some kinds of music is normal. You don't have to like everything.

> Check your answers: Grammar reference, p. 108

7. Match the phrases to make sentences.

1. Learning ___
2. Running ___
3. Singing ___
4. Reading ___
5. Drinking ___
6. Eating ___

a. in a heavy metal band can be hard on your voice.
b. lots of books is a good way to improve your writing skills.
c. a new instrument takes a lot of practice.
d. a lot of fresh fruit and vegetables is good for you.
e. in a marathon requires a lot of athletic ability.
f. soda every day is bad for your teeth.

8. Rewrite the sentences.

1. It's difficult to play three instruments at the same time.
   Playing three instruments at the same time is difficult.

2. It's important to practice for at least an hour a day.
   _____

3. It's not a good idea to take a test on an empty stomach.
   _____

4. It's exciting to have your art in an exhibit.
   _____

5. It isn't cheap to take private music lessons every week.
   _____

6. It's fun to be able to play an instrument well.
   _____

> **Spell it RIGHT!**
> Spelling the -ing forms:
> fix – fix**ing**   work – work**ing**
> If the verb ends in a silent -e, remove the -e and add -ing.
> liv**e** – liv**ing**   danc**e** – danc**ing**
> If a verb ends in a vowel + a consonant, double the consonant.
> hu**g** – hu**gging**   ru**n** – ru**nning**

Speaking: Are you open-minded about music?

9. YOUR TURN Do you agree or disagree with the statements below?

1. I enjoy listening to all kinds of music.
2. Calling some kinds of music "bad" isn't right. If people like it, it's good music for them.
3. Listening to my friends' music is fun, even if it's not my style.
4. I like discovering new bands or singers.

> **Verbs + prepositions + -ing forms (gerunds)**
> You can use the -ing form after some verbs and prepositions.
>
> I want to **apologize for missing** your art exhibition.
>
> Do you **feel like going** to a movie tonight?
>
> This year, Allison needs to **concentrate on studying**, not **hanging out** with her friends.

10. Discuss your answers to Exercise 9 with a partner. Do you agree on everything? Then tell another pair about your partner's answers.

> *Kim likes finding new bands, but she doesn't like all kinds of music. Her sister listens to pop music, and Kim hates that!*

Workbook, pp. 18–19

 3.2 HAVE YOU EVER BEEN TO A CONCERT?

Ready to ROCK?

Conversation: Have you ever been to a concert?

1. **REAL TALK** Watch or listen to the teenagers. Check (✓) the sentences you hear.

   ☐ I've played in some.
   ☐ I prefer going to the cinema (movies).
   ☐ Concert tickets are cheaper than movie tickets.
   ☐ I've been to seven or eight concerts.
   ☐ I love listening to music with a lot of people around.
   ☐ Live music is the best!

2. **YOUR TURN** Have you ever been to a concert? Who did you see? What were the good things and the bad things about the concert?

3. Listen to Mia and Austin talking about a concert. Complete the conversation.

   USEFUL LANGUAGE: Inviting a friend and arranging to meet
   ✓ How about going . . . ?
   That's a good idea.
   Should I ask . . . to take us?
   Sounds good.
   What time should we meet?

   Mia: Hey Austin! ¹ *How about going* to a concert tomorrow?
   Austin: Yeah, why not? Who's playing?
   Mia: A pop rock band called The Sweets. They're a new band. I got free tickets.
   Austin: Sure. ² _____ Where are they playing?
   Mia: The Apollo Club, on Washington Street.
   Austin: OK. ³ _____
   Mia: It starts at 8:30. I think we should go together. How about meeting at my house at 7:30?
   Austin: OK. ⁴ _____
   Mia: Yeah! ⁵ _____ Then maybe my mom could pick us up when it's finished.
   Austin: OK. See you tomorrow, then.

4. Practice the conversation with a partner.

5. **YOUR TURN** Work with a partner. Take turns inviting your friend and arranging to meet. Use the ideas below or your own ideas. Use the conversation in Exercise 3 as a model.

   Concert 1
   The Roots Boyz (reggae)
   The Hacienda Club
   1315 Second Avenue
   Doors open: 8:00 p.m.

   Concert 2
   Live concert with Don't Be Shy (pop rock)
   The Black Bee Soul Club
   2580 Lake Street
   Doors open: 8:30 p.m.

FANTASTIC FREE CONCERT

I just came back from a fantastic free concert. It was in a park about three kilometers from my house, and there was a great atmosphere. There were hundreds of young people there, dancing and enjoying themselves. There were about five bands, but the best one was Hurricane. They're from Cleveland, Ohio, and they play a mixture of lots of different styles, from folk and rock to reggae and blues. I loved listening to the singer (Layla Smith). She has a really amazing voice, and the guitarists and drummer played together really well. They just recorded a CD, and I want to get it! Seeing them play live was great. If you get the chance to see them, go for it! ☺
–Alba

Reading to write: A blog post about a concert

6. Look at the picture and read Alba's blog about a concert. Did she enjoy it?

   ● *Focus on* **CONTENT**
   When you write about a concert, you can include this information:
   - Where it was
   - The audience
   - Who played
   - The styles of music
   - Information about the band(s)
   - Why you liked or didn't like the music

7. Read Alba's blog again. Make notes on the items in the Focus on Content box.

   ● *Focus on* **LANGUAGE**
   Singular and plural forms of *be*
   There **was** a great atmosphere. The best band **was** Hurricane. They (the band members) **are** from Cleveland, Ohio.

8. Find more examples of singular and plural forms of *be* in the blog post.

9. Complete the sentences with the present or past form of the verb *be*.

   1. In my opinion, they ___*are*___ the best rock band on the planet!
   2. There _____ a lot of people at the concert last night, from age 15 to 50.
   3. Most of the people here at the concert tonight _____ obviously big fans of the group, singing every song!
   4. The audience at last night's show _____ tiny, so there _____ (not) a very good atmosphere.
   5. The band _____ (not) famous right now, but I think they will be soon.
   6. All the musicians _____ very professional, but the music _____ (not) usually very exciting.

 Writing: A blog post about a concert

▢ **PLAN**
Plan a blog post about a concert you've been to. Use the list in the Focus on Content box and make notes.

▢ **WRITE**
Write your blog post. Use your notes from Exercise 7 to help you. Write about 120 words.

▢ **CHECK**
Can you say "yes" to these questions?

- Is the information from the Focus on Content box in your writing?
- Did you get all the verbs in the correct singular or plural forms?

A Temporary DESERT CITY

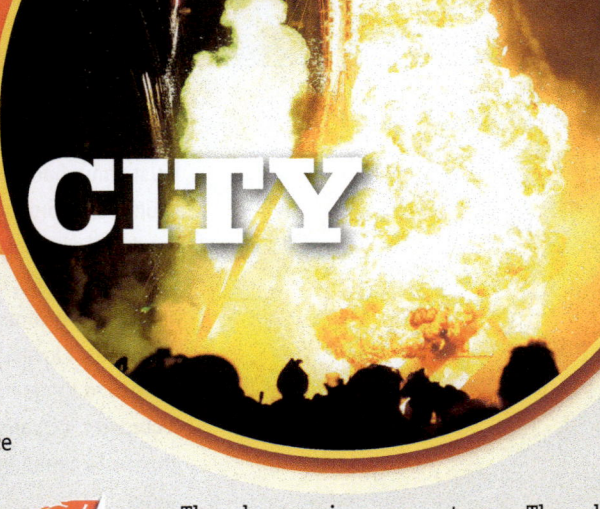

So, some friends have just given you tickets to the Burning Man festival, but you're not sure what to expect. Read these frequently asked questions to find out more:

1 _____ It's a community arts festival. It takes place every year for a week at the end of August in the Black Rock Desert in Nevada, in the US. More than 60,000 people went last year. Volunteers create a community in the desert called Black Rock City. They build everything themselves. The city is in the shape of a giant semi-circle.

2 _____ No, it started in San Francisco, California, in 1986, next to the Golden Gate Bridge. It moved to the desert five years later.

3 _____ Because fire is an important theme of the festival. People build an enormous wooden statue of a person, more than 30 meters tall, and burn it during the festival. They also build and burn lots of other things. Last year, they had an enormous mechanical octopus!

4 _____ They dress up in crazy costumes. They also wear goggles and masks, which protect them from breathing the desert's dust. Besides that, there are a lot of other fun activities. There is usually a balloon chain of 450 different balloons. The chain is one kilometer long and it lights up the sky.

5 _____ When the festival ends, people must take everything away with them and leave the desert exactly as it was before the festival started. The organizers worry about damaging the environment.

6 _____ It's unusual because there aren't any famous bands or celebrities. Hanging out together as a community is what it's all about – everyone is on the same level.

DID YOU KNOW...?

Every August, Black Rock City becomes the third largest city in Nevada – but then it disappears in September!

Culture: The Burning Man festival

1. **Look at the picture of a festival in the US. What do you think people do there?**

2. **Read and listen to the article. Check your answer in Exercise 1.**

3. **Read the article again. Match the questions (a–f) to the answers (1–6) in the article.**
   a. What else do people do at the festival?
   b. Has the festival always taken place there?
   c. What happens after the festival?
   d. What is the Burning Man festival?
   e. How is it different from other festivals?
   f. Why is it called the Burning Man festival?

4. **YOUR TURN** Work with a partner. Ask and answer the questions.
   1. Would you like to go to a festival like Burning Man? Why? / Why not?
   2. Does your school or town have its own festival? What type of festival is it? What can you do there?

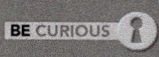 Find out about three different kinds of music. What three countries do the kinds of music come from? (Workbook, p. 77)

3.3 A WORLD OF MUSIC

30 | Unit 3

UNIT 3 REVIEW

Vocabulary

1. Complete the sentences.

comics	exhibition	living statue
✓ graffiti	sculptures	mural

1. There's some new ____graffiti____ on the wall outside the library.
2. I love _____ that are made of stone or metal.
3. There's an amazing _____ in the cafeteria at school. It covers one long wall.
4. My brother is a big fan of superhero _____. He buys a lot of them.
5. I went to an _____ of modern paintings last weekend.
6. One of my friends makes a little money on weekends as a _____. He paints his body silver and wears all silver clothes.

Grammar

2. Write sentences with the simple present and the -ing form of the verb.

1. my aunt / like / play / the guitar
   My aunt likes playing the guitar.
2. Mark and David / hate / sing / in music class
   _____
3. the president of the company / not mind / walk / to work
   _____
4. I / love / practice / the piano
   _____
5. the artist / enjoy / paint / by the river
   _____
6. the festival's participants / not like / sit / in the rain
   _____

3. Complete the sentences.

1. My friends and I talk about ____making____ a music video, but we never do it. (make)
2. _____ a lot is important if you want to become a good musician. (practice)
3. _____ in big festivals is fun, but not everyone likes it. (participate)
4. Did you decide against _____ to play the saxophone? (learn)
5. In my opinion, _____ graffiti on walls is a terrible thing to do. (paint)
6. My father isn't thinking about _____ abroad this year. (travel)

Useful language

4. Complete the conversation.

| What time | ✓ going | Should I | good idea | Sure |

Kyle: Hey Jenna. How about ¹____going____ to a street festival with me?

Jenna: A street festival? Where?

Kyle: Downtown. There will be lots of people playing music on the street for free. There's going to be lots of food there, too. I really want to go.

Jenna: ²_____. Sounds great! ³_____ should we meet?

Kyle: It's from 12:00 p.m. to midnight. How about going for lunch, around 1:00?

Jenna: That's good. ⁴_____ ask my mom to take us?

Kyle: That's a ⁵_____ ! She doesn't mind taking us, does she?

Jenna: No, I don't think so. She might want to see the festival, too.

Kyle: Perfect. See you at 1:00, then?

Jenna: Yes. See you then!

PROGRESS CHECK: Now I can . . .
- ☐ talk about visual arts.
- ☐ express my likes and dislikes.
- ☐ discuss music.
- ☐ make invitations and arrangements.
- ☐ write about a concert that I've been to.
- ☐ discuss a cultural event.

CLIL PROJECT

3.4 ART IN PERSPECTIVE, p. 117

4 Sign Me UP!

Discovery EDUCATION

BE CURIOUS

- The Age of Discovery
- What's the most exciting thing you've ever done?
- Fun in Australia

1. Describe what you see in this picture.
2. How does this picture make you feel?
3. Do you think this kind of sport would be fun?

UNIT CONTENTS

Vocabulary Adventure travel; phrasal verbs related to travel
Grammar Present perfect with *already*, *yet*, *just*, and *yes/no* questions; present perfect with *for*, *since*, and *How long . . . ?*
Listening Adventure travel experiences

Vocabulary: Adventure travel

1. Match the phrases with the correct pictures.

1. _c_ go backpacking
2. ___ go on a cruise
3. ___ go ballooning
4. ___ go mountain biking
5. ___ go rafting
6. ___ go on a safari
7. ___ go sailing
8. ___ go to summer camp
9. ___ go rock climbing

2. Listen, check, and repeat.

3. Which of the activities in Exercise 1 involve:
   a. participating in a sport?
   b. sleeping away from home?
   c. using some kind of transportation?

> **Get it RIGHT!**
> We use *go* before activities that end in *-ing*.
> You can **go rafting** near here. NOT:
> ~~You can do rafting around here.~~

Speaking: I'm in!

4. YOUR TURN Work in groups of three or four. Ask and answer the questions and write the results.

How many students . . .	
a. would like to go rafting?	
b. have gone to a summer camp?	
c. would definitely not want to go rock climbing?	
d. have been on a cruise?	
e. are afraid of going ballooning?	
f. have sailed in a small sailboat?	

5. Tell your results to the class. Make a class chart.

> *Twelve people in the class would enjoy going on a cruise.*

> *Twelve? I have fifteen. Fifteen people would enjoy going on a cruise.*

Workbook, p. 22

Reading Anchors Aweigh!; Tipping help!; Five Good Reasons to Visit New Zealand
Conversation Signing up for an adventure activity
Writing An email comparing different customs

Take to THE WAVES

ANCHORS AWEIGH!

"I've never sailed before. This is my first time, and it's an amazing feeling." Sandra, 16, is on the *Stavros S. Niarchos*, a 70-meter sailing ship, with 40 other young sailors. The *Stavros* is an exact copy of the ships that pirates sailed two or three hundred years ago. It belongs to the Tall Ships Youth Trust. The Trust offers sailing trips at realistic prices for teenagers and young adults. Every year, thousands of young people get their first taste of the sea thanks to the Trust. Up to 70 percent of them are disabled or disadvantaged. For everyone, it's a once-in-a-lifetime experience.

Sandra is on a trip from the Azores, in the North Atlantic, to Spain. The trip lasts a week, and they have already been at sea for three days. "We do everything," she explained. "We sail the ship, we cook, we clean, and we take turns keeping watch at night. I never knew there was so much work on a ship!"

Her friend, Emma, 15, has never been on a boat before either. "I haven't adjusted to life at sea yet. It's very different from life on land!"

"We've done some cool stuff," says James, 17. "My favorite part is climbing the mast. It's 30 meters tall! The views are incredible," said James. "We've just seen dolphins and turtles for the first time. We haven't seen any whales yet, but the captain says there are whales near the Spanish coast. This is definitely the best thing I've ever done!"

If you want to know more about the Tall Ships Youth Trust, visit their website at tallships.org.

Reading: An online article

1. Look at the title and the pictures. What kind of trip is it? Are the teenagers working, having fun, or both?

2. Read and listen to the article. Check your answers in Exercise 1.

3. Read the article again. What does each of the numbers refer to?
   1. 70: _____length of the ship in meters_____ ; _____
   2. 40: _____
   3. two or three hundred: _____
   4. thousands: _____
   5. 15: _____
   6. 30: _____

4. **YOUR TURN** Work with a partner. Ask and answer the questions.
   1. What do you think you can learn on a sailing trip like this?
   2. What are two reasons you would enjoy sailing on a boat like this? What are two reasons you wouldn't enjoy it?

   I think you can learn about yourself on a trip like this.

   What do you mean?

DID YOU KNOW...? Over 95,000 people have sailed 1.8 million nautical miles with the Tall Ships Youth Trust.

Grammar: Present perfect with *already*, *yet*, and *just*

5. Complete the chart.

We can use *already* in affirmative sentences in the present perfect.	
I've **already been** at sea for four days.	He _____ _____ **cooked** three meals for the others on the ship.
We can use *yet* in negative sentences in the present perfect.	
They **haven't found** turtles **yet**.	My sister _____ **visited** the ship _____.
Use *just* with the present perfect to say that something happened very recently.	
We've **just seen** dolphins.	I _____ _____ **boarded** the ship.

> Check your answers: Grammar reference, p. 109

6. Look at the chart. Complete the sentences with *already*, *yet*, or *just*.

1. I'm sorry, but the ship has ___*already*___ left. It left about three hours ago.
2. We haven't sailed alone _____.
3. I've _____ seen a whale! Look! Over there!
4. The boat hasn't left the port _____.
5. She's _____ been on three trips this year.
6. I've _____ finished lunch. It was delicious.

Present perfect questions

We can use *yet* in present perfect questions to ask if something has happened before now.

Have you seen any whales **yet**?	Yes, I have. / No, I haven't.
Has the ship arrived in Spain **yet**?	Yes, it has. / No, it hasn't.

7. Complete the conversation with the present perfect. Then listen and check.

A: Are you ready for the trip?
B: Well, sort of. ¹ *I haven't packed everything yet* (I / not pack / everything / yet), but I know what I want to take.
A: Did you print your tickets?
B: No, not yet. ² _____ (Sam / not send / them / yet).
A: ³ _____ (you / do / anything / yet)?
B: Yes! ⁴ _____ (I / already / pack / my clothes).
A: What about your cell phone?
B: ⁵ _____ (I / just / put / my charger / in my bag), but I'm not going to take my tablet. There's no Internet connection on the ship.
A: And your passport?
B: Yes, don't worry, Mom! ⁶ _____ (I / already / check / that). It's in my purse.

Speaking: New experiences

8. YOUR TURN Work with a partner. Look at the activities, and interview each other. Ask your partner five questions using *already*, *yet*, and *just* about what he or she has done so far this year.

burn any food	send a text message to the wrong person
climb in a window	stay up all night
hurt yourself or break a bone	take a hike
lose your keys	wear socks that don't match

> Have you lost your keys yet this year?
>
> Yes, I have. / No, I haven't.

BE CURIOUS Find out about Ferdinand Magellan. Why were Europeans interested in traveling to Asia? (Workbook, p. 78)

Discovery EDUCATION

4.1 THE AGE OF DISCOVERY

Fun? It was INCREDIBLE!

Listening: Adventure travel experiences

1. Look at the pictures of teenagers on vacation in Rocky Mountain National Park, in Colorado. Do their activities look like fun to you?

2. Listen to three short conversations with some of the teenagers in the pictures. Which sentence best summarizes how they feel about the trip?
   a. They all love everything about their trips.
   b. They think Rocky Mountain National Park is really boring.
   c. They like some of the things they're doing more than other things.

3. Listen again. Answer the questions.
   1. How long has Lily been at the national park? What has she just finished doing?
   2. Does Evan love backpacking? Where did he go yesterday afternoon?
   3. How long has Katie been a rock climber? Which of Katie's family members is with her?

Vocabulary: Phrasal verbs related to travel

4. Complete the sentences with the correct phrasal verbs. Then listen and check your answers.

✓ come back	look around	make sure
find out	look forward to	take off
give up	look out	

   1. I really, really want to ____come back____ here!
   2. _____ – that wall is going to fall down any minute!
   3. You played a good game, and I can't possibly beat you. I _____.
   4. Fasten your seat belts. The plane is about to _____.
   5. I _____ going on vacation this year.
   6. I like to _____ about new trails.
   7. You need to _____ to check your equipment.
   8. Let's have lunch up there and _____ a little.

5. **YOUR TURN** Work with a partner. Ask and answer the questions.
   1. What is something you look forward to doing in the next year?
   2. What are two things you make sure to do before you go to school every day?
   3. After tourists visit your city, what is something that they want to come back and do again?
   4. Before you visit a new place, do you like to find out all about it first?
   5. When you feel tired or you want to give up, what do you do?
   6. When you go to the mall with your friends, do you know exactly what you want, or do you prefer to just go and look around for a while?

   I look forward to going rafting. It sounds super fun!

Grammar: Present perfect with *for* and *since*

6. Complete the chart.

Use the present perfect with *for* or *since* for past actions and events continuing into the present.	
Use *for* with a period of time such as a week, two months, or five years.	
I've been here for three days.	He _____ worked at the rafting company _____ a month.
Use *since* with a specific date or time.	
They _____ been here _____ last Wednesday.	She's lived in Colorado since 2010.

> Check your answers: Grammar reference, p. 109

7. Complete the sentences with *for* or *since*.

1. She's led safari tours every month _____ last November.
2. We've been backpacking in the park _____ Friday.
3. He hasn't gone on a cruise _____ three years, but he loves them.
4. We've played football together _____ 2011.
5. I've lived in Colorado _____ four years.
6. They've looked forward to this vacation _____ a long time.

8. Complete the conversation with the correct words.

| ballooning | for | ✓ How | since |
| been | have | long | yet |

Riley: ¹___How___ long have you lived in Turkey?
Noah: Since 2008. I moved here with my family. How ²_____ have you been here?
Riley: Only ³_____ three weeks. I'm on vacation with my aunt and uncle.
Noah: Cool. How long ⁴_____ you been in Istanbul?
Riley: Only a few days.
Noah: Have you been to Cappadocia ⁵_____?
Riley: No, but we're going to go there tomorrow. Have you ⁶_____ there?
Noah: Yeah, it's fantastic. You can go ⁷_____.
Riley: Really? That's cool!
Noah: Yeah. My family has done it once a year ⁸_____ we moved here. I love it.

How long . . . ? and the present perfect

Use **How long** and the present perfect to ask about the duration of an action or event.

How long have you lived in San Diego? (since 2008 / for 12 years)

How long has she been on the ship? (since July / for three months)

Say it RIGHT!

When you answer questions with *How long . . . ?*, say the time words with more emphasis than the rest of the sentence. Listen and repeat the question and answer.
How long have you lived in Buenos Aires?
*I've lived here for **three years**.*

Speaking: I can't wait to do it again!

9. YOUR TURN Work with a partner. Choose three activities, and ask if your partner has ever done them. Then ask additional questions to continue the conversation.

| fly in an airplane | go rock climbing | go to summer camp | travel to Africa |
| go ballooning | go sailing | travel by ship | travel to the US |

> Have you ever traveled to the US?
>> Yes, I have.
> How long were you there?

Workbook, pp. 24–25

REAL TALK 4.2 WHAT'S THE MOST EXCITING THING YOU'VE EVER DONE?

No experience NEEDED!

Conversation: No experience needed!

1. **REAL TALK** Watch or listen to the teenagers. Check (✓) the things you hear.

   ☐ been on a roller coaster
   ☐ gone camping in the snow
   ☐ jumped off a tall rock
   ☐ skied on a black ski run
   ☐ gone ballooning in the desert
   ☐ gone canyoning
   ☐ played in a concert
   ☐ walked behind a waterfall

2. **YOUR TURN** What's the most exciting thing you've ever done? Tell your partner.

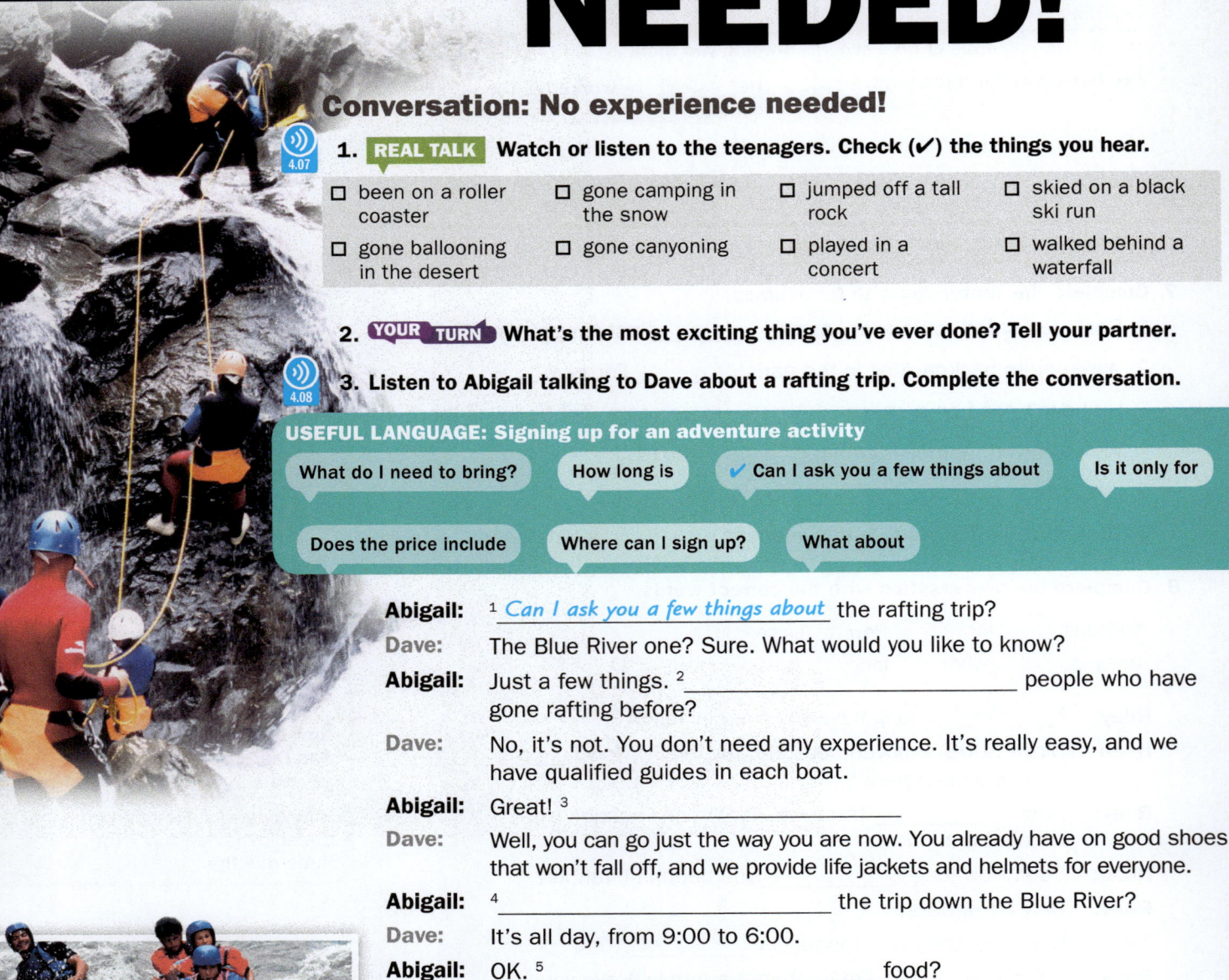

3. Listen to Abigail talking to Dave about a rafting trip. Complete the conversation.

> **USEFUL LANGUAGE: Signing up for an adventure activity**
>
> What do I need to bring?   How long is   ✓ Can I ask you a few things about   Is it only for
>
> Does the price include   Where can I sign up?   What about

Abigail: ¹ *Can I ask you a few things about* the rafting trip?

Dave: The Blue River one? Sure. What would you like to know?

Abigail: Just a few things. ² _____ people who have gone rafting before?

Dave: No, it's not. You don't need any experience. It's really easy, and we have qualified guides in each boat.

Abigail: Great! ³ _____

Dave: Well, you can go just the way you are now. You already have on good shoes that won't fall off, and we provide life jackets and helmets for everyone.

Abigail: ⁴ _____ the trip down the Blue River?

Dave: It's all day, from 9:00 to 6:00.

Abigail: OK. ⁵ _____ food?

Dave: Food is included in the price.

Abigail: ⁶ _____ transportation?

Dave: Yes. We take you to the river and drop you off back here when the trip is finished. We handle everything, so you can just enjoy the adventure.

Abigail: It sounds really fun. ⁷ _____

Dave: Right here!

4. Practice the conversation with a partner.

5. **YOUR TURN** Work with a partner. Take turns asking about the activities below.

Activity 1	Activity 2
Sailing in the ocean with qualified instructors. We provide: life jacket, hot drinks on Belle Island You bring: swimsuit and towel, warm clothes Transportation from hotel to beach not included. Morning (9:00–12:00) or afternoon (3:00–6:00)	Rock climbing on Red Mountain with qualified instructors. We provide: rock-climbing equipment, helmets, transportation to Red Mountain You bring: appropriate clothing for weather, good tennis shoes or rock-climbing shoes All day 10:00 to 5:00

38 | Unit 4

To: audrey@net.cup.org
From: jean-claude@net.cup.org
Subject: Tipping help!

Dear Audrey,

How are you doing? I wonder if you could help me with something. I was recently on a mountain biking trip in Europe with some Americans. When we ate in restaurants, I did what we do in France: I either left a small tip, or I didn't leave a tip at all. Not only did the Americans leave a big tip (sometimes 20 percent or more of the bill!), but they also thought I was rude because I didn't. I can't believe Americans give the waiter that much money each time they eat out. Next month, I'm going to visit these friends in California for a biking trip there. You're American, but you've lived in France. What is the correct thing to do when we eat out?

Sincerely,
Jean-Claude

Dear Jean-Claude,

Wow! I'm not surprised you're confused. Although people tip waiters in both France and in the United States, tipping practices are different. In France, the tip – a service fee – is included in the bill. When I've been in France, I've sometimes left a few coins, or I've left as much as a euro for a meal. In the United States, however, waiters make very small salaries, and service is not included in the bill. Waiters depend on tips to survive, so Americans always leave a tip. Be prepared to add 15 to 20 percent to everything you order in a restaurant in the United States. And have fun biking!

Sincerely,
Audrey

Reading to write: An email comparing different customs

6. Look at the picture. Do you know what the money we leave a server in a restaurant is called? Read the emails and find out.

> ### Focus on CONTENT
> **Comparing**
> When you're comparing two different customs, be sure to compare the same topic for both places. Choose one topic at a time and compare how each place deals with the topic.

7. Look at the emails again. Answer the questions.

1. What topic is Jean-Claude writing about?
2. What is the custom in France?
3. What is the custom in the United States?

> ### Focus on LANGUAGE
> **Conjunctions**
> Use conjunctions to show relationships between ideas.
> both . . . and
> either . . . or
> not only . . . but also
> however
> although

8. Find one example of each conjunction in the emails.

Workbook, pp. 26–27

Writing: An email comparing different customs

PLAN
Think of something from your country that might be confusing to someone from a different country. This could be greeting people, hand gestures, things people do (or don't do) in public, the things people do to have fun, or unique foods.

WRITE
Write an email to an imaginary friend from another country. Use the email above to help you. Write about 120 words.

CHECK
Can you say "yes" to these questions?

- Is the information from the Focus on Content box in your writing? Are you comparing the same thing in both cultures?

- Did you use conjunctions to show relationships between ideas?

Five Good Reasons to Visit NEW ZEALAND

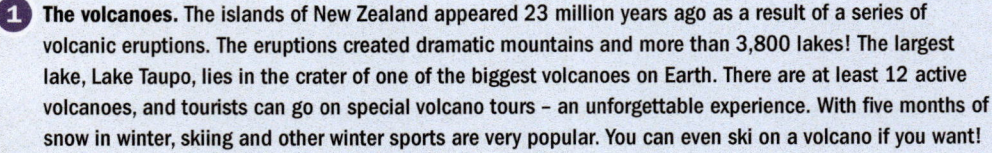

a

b

c

d

e

1. **The volcanoes.** The islands of New Zealand appeared 23 million years ago as a result of a series of volcanic eruptions. The eruptions created dramatic mountains and more than 3,800 lakes! The largest lake, Lake Taupo, lies in the crater of one of the biggest volcanoes on Earth. There are at least 12 active volcanoes, and tourists can go on special volcano tours – an unforgettable experience. With five months of snow in winter, skiing and other winter sports are very popular. You can even ski on a volcano if you want!

2. **The forests.** More than 30 percent of New Zealand is forest. Some of the forests have remained unchanged for millions of years. They're old, beautiful, and mysterious! They have made New Zealand a perfect choice for film directors. Did you know that the forests, lakes, and mountains were the settings for several important Hollywood movies like *The Hobbit*, *The Lord of the Rings*, and *The Chronicles of Narnia*?

3. **The beaches.** New Zealand has more than 6,000 kilometers of coastline. The beaches are long and sandy, and the conditions are perfect for water sports. Kayaking, diving, surfing, and sailing are all popular sports with locals and visitors. You can't visit New Zealand without visiting at least one of its fantastic beaches!

4. **The whales and dolphins.** Half of the world's whale and dolphin population lives in the seas around New Zealand. Kaikoura, on the South Island, is one of the best whale-watching spots in the world. If you've never seen a whale up close, this is your chance, and you shouldn't miss it.

5. **The culture.** Humans have only lived on the islands for about 1,000 years. The first people to arrive were islanders from Eastern Polynesia, called Maori. Today, about 15 percent of the population of New Zealand is Maori. Their culture and their customs developed into the Maori way of life. Maori language, literature, music, dance, sports, and even TV are all important in New Zealand. If you're in New Zealand, you should visit a *marae* – a Maori community facility – or even learn to speak the language.

Culture: New Zealand

1. Look at the pictures of different outdoor activities that you can see or do in New Zealand. Answer the questions.
   1. Have you ever done any of the activities?
   2. Which of the activities would you like to try?

2. Read and listen to the article. Match the photos from Exercise 1 to the reasons for visiting New Zealand.
   1. ____   2. ____   3. ____   4. ____   5. ____

3. Read the article again. Find the numbers in the box in the article and explain what they refer to.

23 million years ago	30 percent	1,000 years
3,800	millions of years	15 percent
12	6,000 kilometers	
five months	half	

4. **YOUR TURN** Work with a partner. Ask and answer the questions.
   1. Would you like to go to New Zealand? Why? / Why not?
   2. What outdoor activities can you do in and around your town or city?
   3. Do you have a favorite outdoor activity? If so, what is it? Why do you like it?

DID YOU KNOW…?
The human population of New Zealand is four million. The sheep population is 36 million!

BE CURIOUS
Find out about some of the things that make Australia unusual. What unusual sport happens in Alice Springs? (Workbook, p. 79)

Discovery EDUCATION
4.3 FUN IN AUSTRALIA

UNIT 4 REVIEW

Vocabulary

1. Complete the sentences with the activities.

| go backpacking | go on a cruise | go sailing |
| go ballooning | go on a safari | ✓ go to summer camp |

1. If you _go to summer camp,_ you'll make friends and learn new skills with kids your own age.
2. Let's _____! My father bought a new boat and he wants to go out on the lake.
3. We're going to _____ while we're in South Africa. I hope we see lions.
4. I'd love to _____. It must be fun to be on a big ship with swimming pools!
5. My brother wants to _____ for four days. I don't understand why because he hates walking. He won't even walk our dog!
6. I'm going to _____ in New Mexico again next week. I love floating along in the air, quietly looking down at the ground.

Grammar

2. Seth and Mary are planning a weekend trip to the mountains. Write sentences or questions using the present perfect.

1. Seth and Mary / buy a guidebook / already
   Seth and Mary have already bought a guidebook.
2. Mary / not reserve a place to camp / yet
   _____
3. Seth / pack his backpack / yet ?
   _____
4. Mary / check the weather report / just
   _____
5. They / not fill the car with gas / yet
   _____

3. Write *for* or *since* to complete the phrases.

1. _for_ a long time
2. _____ a year
3. _____ January 10
4. _____ Monday
5. _____ 10 days
6. _____ two weeks

Useful language

4. Complete the conversation.

| about transportation | do I | include | Where |
| ✓ Can I | how | Is it only | |

Nick: Hi! ¹ _Can I_ ask you a few things about the mountain biking trip?

Gabriella: Yeah. What would you like to know?

Nick: I've done a lot of biking, but I haven't gone mountain biking yet. ² _____ for people who have already done it?

Gabriella: No, this is on beginner trails. It's easy.

Nick: OK. What ³_____ need to bring?

Gabriella: Nothing. Just wear tennis shoes and comfortable clothes. We supply the helmets and the bikes.

Nick: Cool. What ⁴_____ to the start of the trail? Do you drive us there?

Gabriella: No, but there's a parking lot right there. You can drive and park your car there and meet us. Or you can walk. It isn't far at all.

Nick: OK. And ⁵_____ long is the trip?

Gabriella: All day, from 9:00 a.m. to 4:00 p.m.

Nick: Does the price ⁶_____ lunch?

Gabriella: Yes, and two snacks.

Nick: Cool! ⁷_____ can I sign up?

PROGRESS CHECK: Now I can . . .

☐ talk about adventure travel.
☐ ask and answer questions about personal experiences.
☐ ask and answer questions about the duration of activities.
☐ talk about signing up for an adventure activity.
☐ write about different customs.
☐ discuss reasons to visit a place.

5 Yikes!

Discovery EDUCATION™
BE CURIOUS

- Creepy Creatures
- What are you afraid of? 
- Calendars of the Ancient Maya 
- City or Country? 

1. Describe what you see in this picture.
2. How does this picture make you feel?
3. What kinds of things make you feel afraid?

UNIT CONTENTS

Vocabulary Fears; *-ed* and *-ing* adjective endings
Grammar Future review; first conditional; modals of probability – *must, can't, may, might, could*
Listening Conversations at an amusement park

Vocabulary: Fears

1. Match the photos (a–h) with the words.

1. __e__ flying
2. _____ heights
3. _____ the dark
4. _____ elevators
5. _____ insects
6. _____ birds
7. _____ clowns
8. _____ snakes

2. Listen, check, and repeat.

3. Match the comments about fears to the words in Exercise 1.

1. "I'm worried they might fly in through an open window and scratch me, or they might get into my hair!" _____
2. "I can't look out the windows of tall buildings. I get dizzy and have to sit down!" _____
3. "They're supposed to be funny, but their faces are really scary!" _____
4. "I always take the stairs." _____
5. "I sleep with a light on every night." _____
6. "I prefer to travel by train or car than by plane." _____
7. "I hate it when one flies into my face! I don't care how small it is, I always jump." _____
8. "I'm terrified when I'm out in the woods. I carry a stick and watch the grass for them." _____

Speaking: Reactions to fear

4. YOUR TURN Talk to three people in your class. Answer the questions below.

1. Do you know anyone who has any of these fears or other common ones?
2. How does the fear change his or her behavior?

Person	Fear	Behavior changes
Anna	flying	drives long distances to avoid planes

5. Tell your partner about the people you know and their fears.

My mother has a fear of flying. She drives really long distances to avoid going on a plane!

▶ Workbook, p. 30

Reading Ask Maria; Afraid to fly!; Superstitions? Who Needs Them?!
Conversation Expressing disbelief
Writing An email to a friend about plans and problems

HELP!

Ask MARIA

Today we're going to look at fears and phobias. Everybody's afraid of something – elevators, insects, snakes – and famous people have fears, too. Did you know that Daniel Radcliffe is scared of clowns, Orlando Bloom is scared of pigs, and Nicole Kidman is scared of butterflies? For Justin Timberlake, it's spiders, and for Matt Damon, snakes. For most people, these fears aren't very important. However, when a fear becomes a phobia – an extreme and uncontrollable fear – it can cause serious problems.

Carlos, 14 (California)

"I can't sleep at night without a light, and sometimes it can be embarrassing. Next week, I'm traveling to New York on a school trip, and I'm going to share a room with other students. I don't want them to think I'm a baby! Please help. I'm really worried!"

Don't be embarrassed. Did you know that Keanu Reeves is afraid of the dark? And no one says he's a baby! Don't worry about what other people will think of you. Just tell your roommates that you want the light on at night like it's the most normal thing in the world.

Isabella, 13 (Florida)

"My uncle is getting married next month, and my mom, my dad, and I are going to the wedding – in Las Vegas! The problem is that I'm terrified of flying, and the flight to Las Vegas takes four and a half hours. What am I going to do?"

Lots of people are afraid of flying. Jennifer Aniston, for example, hates planes, so you're in good company! Try to relax before the flight. If you get some exercise, you'll feel tired, and then maybe you can sleep. Listen to your favorite music. When you feel nervous, close your eyes, and take long, deep breaths. If you do just one or two of these things, you'll be fine!

Reading: An advice column

1. Look at the famous people in the pictures. What do you think they're afraid of?

2. Read and listen to the online advice column and check your answers to the question in Exercise 1.

3. Read the advice column again and answer the questions.
   1. What is the difference between a fear and a phobia?
   2. Why does Isabella have to travel?
   3. What is Maria's advice to Isabella?
   4. Why does Carlos have to travel?
   5. What is Carlos worried about?
   6. What is Maria's advice to Carlos?

4. **YOUR TURN** Work with a partner. Ask and answer the questions.
   1. Do you think Maria gave good advice?
   2. Do you know of any other famous people who have fears or phobias? What are their fears?
   3. Do you think it's easy to help people with phobias? Why or why not?

DID YOU KNOW…?

Arachnophobia – fear of spiders – is the most common phobia. Fifty percent of all women suffer from arachnophobia.

Grammar: Future review – *will, be going to*, present continuous

5. Complete the chart.

> *Use* will, be going to, *and the present continuous to talk about the future.*
> *Use* will *for actions and events that we decide to do in the moment of speaking.*
> Are you going running now? I _____ (go) with you.
> *Use* going to *for planned actions and events. They may be in the near future or in a more distant future time.*
> My brother and his friends are _____ (be) in different schools next year.
> *Use the present continuous for planned actions and events, usually in the very near future.*
> Lauren _____ (have) dinner with her mother tonight.
> *Be going to is used much more than* will *in conversation.*

> Check your answers: Grammar reference, p. 110

6. Choose the best option.

1. Your bag looks heavy. Give it to me. I **will / am going to** help you carry it.
2. What **are you doing / will you do** this weekend? Do you have plans?
3. My friends can't go out tonight. They **will / are going to** study for the big math test.
4. What **are we having / will we have** for dinner tonight?
5. If all of you are going dancing now, I think I **will / am going to** go to bed. I'm tired.
6. Dave and Julianne **will / are going to** take a trip to Chile next year.

7. Complete the sentences with a verb from the box. Use *will* for first conditional sentences. For other sentences, use *be going to*.

| go | see | study |
| get | stay | ✓ take |

1. I _am going to take_ an English course in New York next summer.
2. If my brother doesn't go to college, he _____ a job.
3. My best friend _____ harder next semester. Her grades are just terrible now.
4. If I don't have any plans this weekend, I _____ home and watch TV.
5. We _____ Julie tonight.
6. Your friends _____ to camp this summer.

> **First conditional**
>
> *Use first conditional sentences to talk about things that may happen in the future.*
>
> If you don't go to bed soon, you **will** be tired tomorrow.
>
> If you hurry up, we **will** have time to see a movie tonight.
>
> If you wear your boots, your feet **won't** get wet in the rain.

Speaking: *I'm going to . . .*

8. YOUR TURN Work with a partner. Ask and answer the questions.

1. What are you going to do when you finish high school?
2. What are you doing this weekend?

> What are you going to do when you finish high school?

> I think I'm going to go to college. But maybe I'll travel for a few months first.

BE CURIOUS Find out about king cobras. Are you scared of snakes? Why or why not? (Workbook, p. 80)

Discovery EDUCATION

5.1 CREEPY CREATURES

Workbook, p. 31

Scared? I was TERRIFIED!

Listening: Conversations at an amusement park

1. Work with a partner. Look at the picture on the left. How do you think the people on the roller coaster feel? Do you like roller coasters? Why? / Why not?

2. Listen to two conversations between a group of friends at an amusement park. How do Alyssa and Bruno feel (a) at the beginning of the day, and (b) at the end of the day?

3. Listen again. Choose the correct answer to each question.

   Conversation 1:
   1. Which ride is Alyssa scared of?
      a. The Scream Machine   b. The Colossus   c. The Tidal Wave
   2. Why doesn't Bruno like the Tidal Wave?
      a. The line is short.   b. He doesn't like the water.   c. He wants to swim.
   3. Why does Colin suggest starting with The Scream Machine?
      a. The line is short.   b. It's very scary.   c. It's a lot of fun.

   Conversation 2:
   4. What was Colin's favorite ride?
      a. The Colossus   b. The Tidal Wave   c. The Scream Machine
   5. What was the problem at the end of the day?
      a. They missed the bus.   b. They spent a lot of money.   c. There's nothing to eat.

Vocabulary: -ed and -ing adjective endings

4. Look at the pictures and read the Notice it box. Circle the correct adjectives. Then listen and check your answers.
   1. The movie we saw last night was **terrified / terrifying**!
   2. Yesterday, we looked at the physics of roller coasters in class. It was very **interested / interesting**.
   3. I was completely **surprised / surprising** when I got the present you sent me.
   4. We went on a 20-kilometer walk in the country last weekend. It was **exhausted / exhausting**!
   5. I'm **confused / confusing**. Do we have a test tomorrow or not?
   6. My brother fell down in the cafeteria yesterday. Everyone saw him, and he felt really **embarrassed / embarrassing**.
   7. After a three-week vacation at the beach, I felt really **relaxed / relaxing**.
   8. Some reality shows on TV are really **disgusted / disgusting**.

5. **YOUR TURN** Write six true sentences about your feelings and beliefs using the cues below. Then tell your partner.

interested in	_____ is / are disgusting
embarrassed by	_____ is / are exhausting
terrified of	_____ is / are confusing

   NOTICE IT
   Use -ed adjective endings to say how you feel. Use -ing adjective endings to talk about something or someone that causes that feeling.

I was terrified.

The ride was terrifying.

Grammar: Modals of probability – *must, can't, may, might, could*

6. Complete the chart.

Use *must* for something you're almost certain of.	Use *can't* for something you believe is impossible.	Use *may*, *might*, and *could* for something that you believe is possible.
You have to be 14 or older to go on that ride. It _____ **be** really terrifying.	Ralph doesn't speak French, so he _____ **be** from France.	I don't know where your sister is, but she _____ **be** upstairs. I _____ **not go** to the barbecue because I haven't finished my homework. My dog doesn't want to eat. He _____ **be** sick.

> Check your answers: Grammar reference, p. 110

7. Choose the correct answers.

1. The roller coaster **must / can't** be fun. There are lots of people in line.
2. You **must / can't** expect to win the lottery. Millions of people play it every week.
3. You **must / can't** be really tired. You fell asleep twice during the movie.
4. My neighbor **must / can't** make a lot of money. He's always taking expensive trips.
5. She **must / can't** be a good student. She misses school at least once a week.
6. I **must / can't** be late. I left an hour early!

8. Complete the sentences with *must, can't,* or *could*.

1. You haven't eaten all day? Let me make you a snack. You _____ be hungry!
2. My mom _____ be at work or at the mall. She's not here.
3. We _____ fail the test. The teacher said we could look at our books.
4. Your brother _____ get hurt if he's not careful.
5. That guy over there is speaking French. He _____ be the new student from Canada.
6. You drank three glasses of water 15 minutes ago. You _____ be thirsty again.

> **Get it RIGHT!**
>
> Don't use *must* to discuss probability in the future.
> *If you don't go to bed now, you* **will** *be tired tomorrow.* NOT: *If you don't go to bed now, you* **must** *be tired tomorrow.*

Speaking: Surprising situations

9. YOUR TURN Read the situations below. Why do you think they're happening? Discuss with a partner. Be creative, and use *must, can't, might, may,* and *could*.

Situation 1: John bought a new bike last week, but he isn't using it. He's walking to school this morning.

Situation 2: Sean is a great athlete. He loves to play basketball, baseball, and football, but he isn't playing any sports at school this year.

Situation 3: Alicia has an important test in school tomorrow, but right now she's on a plane, going to Japan.

> John's bike must be broken.
>> It can't be broken. It's new.
>>> Well, it could have a flat tire. Maybe . . .

Workbook, pp. 32-33

REAL TALK 5.2 WHAT ARE YOU AFRAID OF?

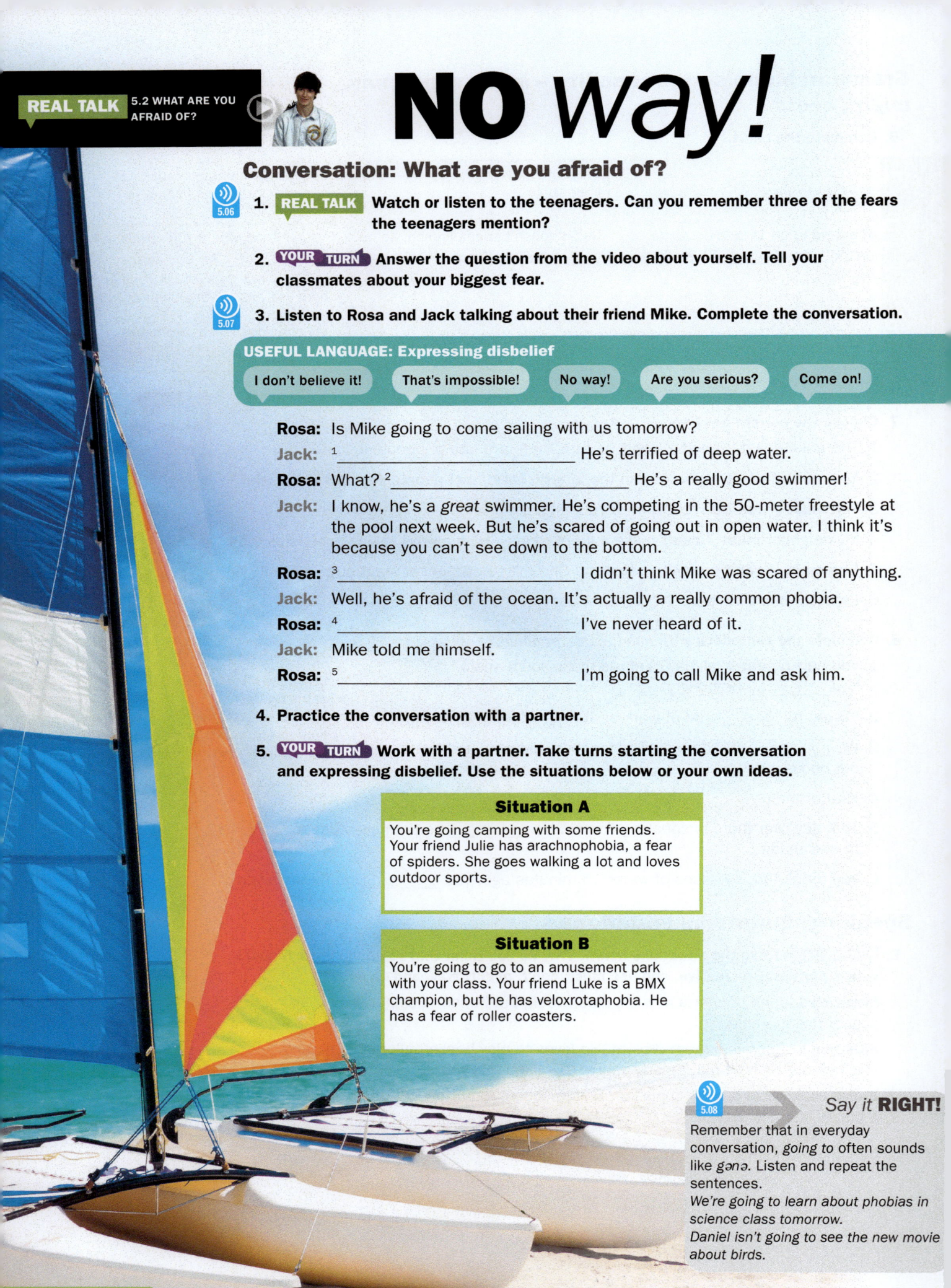

NO way!

Conversation: What are you afraid of?

1. **REAL TALK** Watch or listen to the teenagers. Can you remember three of the fears the teenagers mention?

2. **YOUR TURN** Answer the question from the video about yourself. Tell your classmates about your biggest fear.

3. Listen to Rosa and Jack talking about their friend Mike. Complete the conversation.

USEFUL LANGUAGE: Expressing disbelief

I don't believe it!   That's impossible!   No way!   Are you serious?   Come on!

Rosa: Is Mike going to come sailing with us tomorrow?
Jack: [1]_____ He's terrified of deep water.
Rosa: What? [2]_____ He's a really good swimmer!
Jack: I know, he's a *great* swimmer. He's competing in the 50-meter freestyle at the pool next week. But he's scared of going out in open water. I think it's because you can't see down to the bottom.
Rosa: [3]_____ I didn't think Mike was scared of anything.
Jack: Well, he's afraid of the ocean. It's actually a really common phobia.
Rosa: [4]_____ I've never heard of it.
Jack: Mike told me himself.
Rosa: [5]_____ I'm going to call Mike and ask him.

4. Practice the conversation with a partner.

5. **YOUR TURN** Work with a partner. Take turns starting the conversation and expressing disbelief. Use the situations below or your own ideas.

Situation A
You're going camping with some friends. Your friend Julie has arachnophobia, a fear of spiders. She goes walking a lot and loves outdoor sports.

Situation B
You're going to go to an amusement park with your class. Your friend Luke is a BMX champion, but he has veloxrotaphobia. He has a fear of roller coasters.

Say it **RIGHT!**
Remember that in everyday conversation, *going to* often sounds like *gənə*. Listen and repeat the sentences.
We're going to learn about phobias in science class tomorrow.
Daniel isn't going to see the new movie about birds.

To: Pete
From: Stefan
Subject: Afraid to fly!

Hi Pete,

Thanks for the email with your news. Now here's my news. Check this out: I'm going to stay with my cousins in Colorado this summer. I'm going with my parents, and the idea is that we'll all go camping together. It's really exciting, but the problem is that we're flying there ☹! I've never been on a plane before, and the truth is, I'm really worried about flying. I don't know what to do! When I think about getting on a plane, I feel tense and start sweating. It's embarrassing. Listen to this: I had to tell my mom, and she said it's just like going on a bus. She told me not to worry. Not very helpful! I want to go by car, but that will take four days. And so, the fact is, I might not go at all because I'm terrified of planes. What do you think I should do?

Sincerely,

Stefan

Reading to write: An email to a friend

6. Read Stefan's email. What is he worried about?

> ⊙ *Focus on* **CONTENT**
> When you write an email about a problem, you can include this information:
> - A greeting (*Hi Mike! Dear Sandra,*)
> - Some personal news
> - What the problem is
> - How you feel about it and why
> - What you have / haven't done about it
> - A question to ask what your friend thinks

7. Read Stefan's email again. What information does he include for each category from the Focus on Content box?

> ⊙ *Focus on* **LANGUAGE**
> **Introducing something**
> *Listen to this:*
> *The idea is (that) . . .*

8. Find examples of the items in the Focus on Language box in Stefan's email. Can you find two other ways of introducing information?

9. Rewrite the sentences using the words given.

1. We're going to Argentina next month. (listen to this)

   Listen to this: We're going to Argentina next month.

2. I'm going to get a dog. (check this out)

   _____

3. A lot of people have phobias about roller coasters. (the fact)

   _____

4. She doesn't want to go. (the truth)

   _____

Workbook, pp. 34–35

Writing: An email to a friend about plans and problems

☐ **PLAN**
Think about a problem or worry you've had recently. It can be about anything: school, homework, your family, fears, phobias, or the future. Then think of someone you could send an email to for help with that problem. Look at the Focus on Content box and make notes about what you'll write.

☐ **WRITE**
Write your email. Use your notes and the language below to help you. Write about 120 words.

Thanks for your email / letter.

The idea is that . . .

It's really exciting / surprising / embarrassing . . .

I feel terrible / confused because . . .

What can I do? / What do you think I should do?

☐ **CHECK**
Check your writing. Can you answer "yes" to these questions?

- Is the information from the Focus on Content box in your email?
- Have you used expressions like *The problem is that* . . . in your email?

Unit 5 | 49

Superstitions? Who Needs Them?!

Many superstitions have been around for thousands of years. For example, some people believe that walking under ladders brings bad luck or finding a horseshoe brings good luck. Some superstitions began recently – for example, many soccer players don't change their socks or underwear while their team is winning.

Lots of people, however, believe strongly that superstitions are silly. They say that believing in superstitions is a way of trying to control things we can't control. They say that superstitions are based on old habits, old customs, and old beliefs. How is it possible that you could have bad luck by opening an umbrella inside a house? Why is the number 13 more dangerous than other numbers?

To prove their point, they have "Anti-Superstition Parties." These are usually held on a Friday the Thirteenth, a date that many people think brings bad luck. At these parties, people break mirrors, walk under ladders, and dance with open umbrellas. And nothing bad happens!

Alan Moore, a Chicago dentist, has gone to several anti-superstition parties. He said, "People must be crazy to believe that the number 7 is lucky or that they could be more successful by putting a horseshoe outside their house." Chelsea Evans, a chef from Dallas, agrees. "I love the parties. I've broken lots of mirrors and my life is going great!"

Culture: Anti-superstition parties

1. **Read the title of the article and look at the picture. What do you think the article is about?**

2. **Read and listen to the article. Check (✓) the things you read and hear about.**

   - ☐ breaking mirrors
   - ☐ black cats
   - ☐ blowing out birthday candles
   - ☐ opening umbrellas
   - ☐ walking under ladders
   - ☐ throwing rice

3. **Read the article again. Are the sentences below true (T) or false (F)?**

   1. All superstitions have a recent origin. ____
   2. Some soccer players are superstitious. ____
   3. Lots of superstitions come from old habits and beliefs. ____
   4. At anti-superstition parties, people are careful to follow old superstitions. ____
   5. Alan and Chelsea are scared to go to anti-superstition parties. ____
   6. Chelsea's life is fine even though she has broken a lot of mirrors. ____

4. **YOUR TURN Work with a partner. Ask and answer the questions.**

   1. What superstitions exist in your country? Do you believe in any of them?
   2. Are there logical or scientific explanations for superstitions?
   3. Have you ever heard of anti-superstition parties? Would you like to go to one?

DID YOU KNOW...?
Fear of the number 13 is called triskaidekaphobia.

BE CURIOUS Find out about ancient Mayan calendars. What happened on Mayan "good days" and "bad days"? (Workbook, p. 81)

Discovery EDUCATION
5.3 CALENDARS OF THE ANCIENT MAYA

UNIT 5 REVIEW

Vocabulary

1. **Write the common fears next to the words they are related to. There are two extra words.**

birds	elevators	heights	snakes
clowns	✓ flying	insects	the dark

   1. airplanes _flying_
   2. tall buildings _____
   3. small spaces _____
   4. poisonous animals _____
   5. no light _____
   6. spiders, beetles, butterflies _____

Grammar

2. **Write sentences or questions with *be going to*. Use contracted forms if possible.**

   1. We / fly / to Japan / tomorrow
      We're going to fly to Japan tomorrow.
   2. Jim / learn / the guitar / next semester
      _____
   3. They / order / pizza / tonight
      _____
   4. She / not use / her computer / this weekend
      _____
   5. I / go to college / when I finish high school
      _____
   6. Danielle / look for / a new job / next year
      _____

3. **Complete the sentences with *must*, *can't*, or *might*.**

   1. Whose suitcase is that? It _____ belong to Erin, but I'm not sure.
   2. I had my wallet just a second ago. It _____ be here somewhere.
   3. Anna _____ be home sick. I saw her at school five minutes ago.
   4. It's so cold outside that it _____ snow tonight.
   5. You _____ be tired yet. We only started walking a few minutes ago.
   6. Daniel isn't answering his phone. It _____ be turned off because he always answers it.

Useful language

4. **Complete the conversation.**

believe it	on
impossible	serious

   Grace: We're going to an amusement park next weekend. Want to come?

   Ryan: No, I'd better not. I always have bad luck when I go to amusement parks.

   Grace: What do you mean?

   Ryan: Every time I go, something bad happens. Last time, I was at the top of a roller coaster and the electricity went out. I sat in the car for 45 minutes.

   Grace: Are you [1]_____?

   Ryan: I'm not joking. And another time, I was on the Spinning Hat ride and the person next to me got sick. It was disgusting!

   Grace: Come [2]_____. Just because you had a few bad things happen doesn't mean something bad will happen every time. That's [3]_____.

   Ryan: No it isn't! And then, last summer, I went with my friends and fell down – I was just walking along – and had to go to the hospital!

   Grace: I don't [4]_____!

   Ryan: It's true! Sorry, but I think I'll just stay home.

PROGRESS CHECK: Now I can . . .
- ☐ identify and discuss common fears.
- ☐ talk about future events.
- ☐ talk about things that are possible and not possible.
- ☐ express disbelief.
- ☐ discuss superstitions.
- ☐ write an email to a friend about plans and problems.

CLIL PROJECT

5.4 CITY OR COUNTRY?, p. 118

Uncover Your Knowledge
UNITS 1–5 Review Game

TEAM 1 START

1. Share an opinion with your teammate and ask him or her to agree with you. Your teammate disagrees with you and explains why.
2. Tell your teammate about a time you felt embarrassed, stressed out, or wonderful.
3. Say three future actions: one you've just decided to do, one for this weekend, and one for next year.
4. Use each of these words in a unique sentence: terrified, interesting, confused, relaxing.
5. Have your teammate tell you two things that are very surprising. Express your disbelief in two ways.
6. Name the top three priorities you have in life, and explain why they are important to you.
7. What do you have to do to get a good grade in English? Tell your teammate, using have to/don't have to.
8. Give examples of three adventure travel activities you want to try.
9. Role-play a conversation with your teammate. Invite him or her to an art exhibit and plan to meet.
10. Say how long you've studied English. Then use a negative statement to tell your teammate the last time you saw a movie in a theater.
11. Describe something you're looking forward to, something you want to find out about, and someplace you want to come back to.

- GRAMMAR
- VOCABULARY
- USEFUL LANGUAGE

INSTRUCTIONS:

- Make teams and choose game pieces.
- Put your game pieces on your team's START.
- Flip a coin to see who goes first.
- Read the first challenge. Can you do it correctly?

    Yes → Continue to the next challenge.

    No → Lose your turn.

The first team to do all of the challenges wins!

TEAM 2 — START

- Use the verbs *learn*, *play*, and *make* as the subjects of three different sentences.
- Name six basic needs that people have.
- Think about a few things you wanted to do last week. Use *already* to talk about something you did, and *yet* to talk about something you haven't done.
- How can you ask someone for information? Give three examples.
- Say two things you did yesterday and two things you used to do in the past but don't do anymore.
- In 30 seconds, name five things people are often afraid of.
- Say one thing you're almost sure about, one thing you think is possible, and one thing you believe is impossible. Use modals of probability.
- Give examples of five types of extreme weather.
- Tell your teammate something you hate doing, something you love doing, and something you don't mind doing.
- Name one type of artwork, one place to see art, and one type of artist.
- Role-play a conversation with your teammate. Ask him or her to help you with something.
- Tell your teammate that studying more would be a good thing for you to do. Say it three different ways, using modals of obligation.
- Imagine you are in a band. What instrument do you play? What other instruments do you have in the band? Give four examples.
- Tell your teammate two things you do every day and two things you are doing right now.

Units 1–5 Review | 53

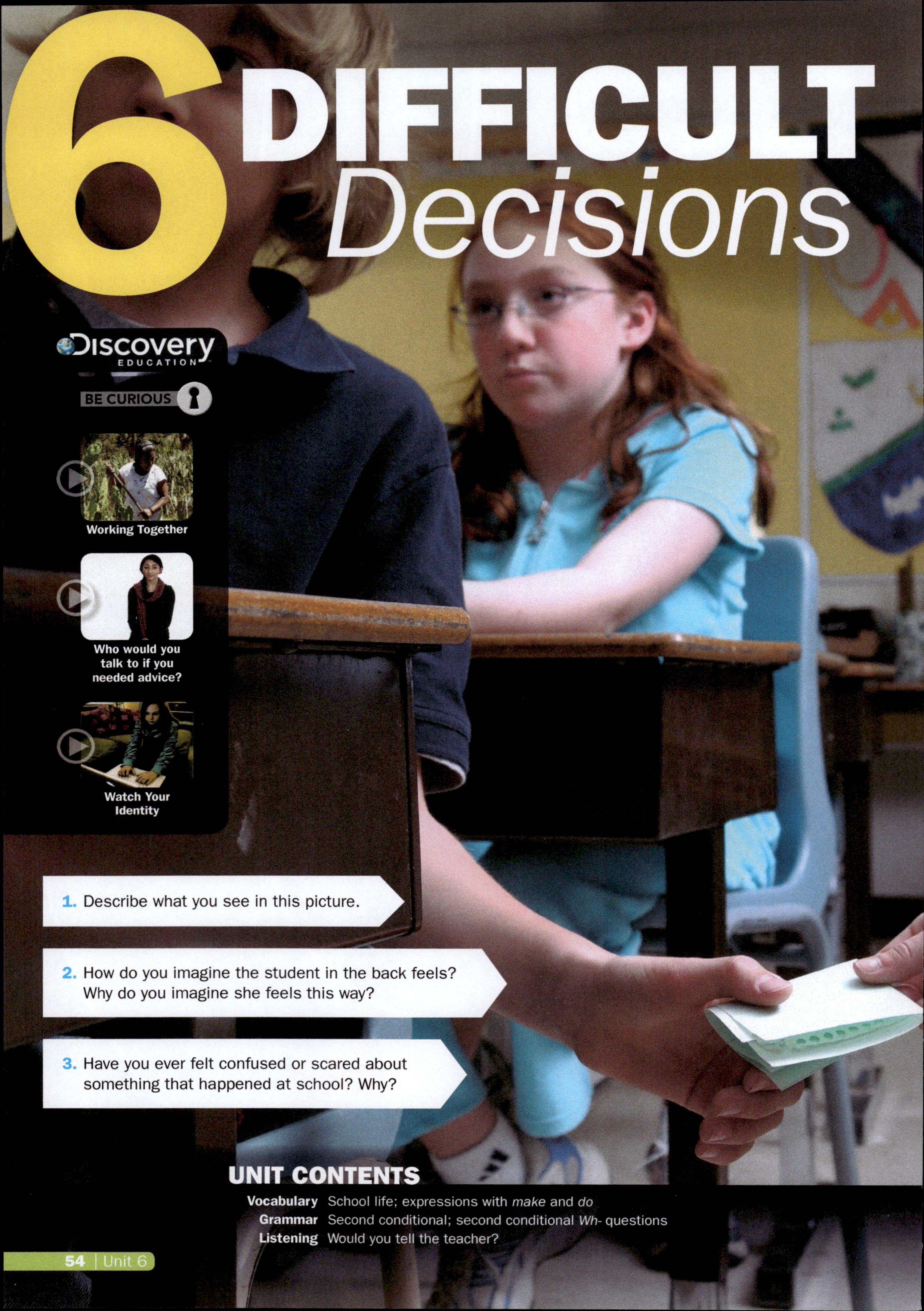

6 DIFFICULT Decisions

Discovery EDUCATION

BE CURIOUS

- Working Together
- Who would you talk to if you needed advice?
- Watch Your Identity

1. Describe what you see in this picture.

2. How do you imagine the student in the back feels? Why do you imagine she feels this way?

3. Have you ever felt confused or scared about something that happened at school? Why?

UNIT CONTENTS

Vocabulary School life; expressions with *make* and *do*
Grammar Second conditional; second conditional *Wh-* questions
Listening Would you tell the teacher?

54 | Unit 6

Vocabulary: School life

1. Read the phrases related to school life. Then circle the correct answers.

being assigned to detention	cheating	wearing a uniform
being punctual	following the dress code	winning a prize
being rude	getting sent to the principal's office	
bullying	getting extra credit	

1. You can _____ in English if you read two books over the vacation.
   a. get sent to the principal's office   (b. get extra credit)

2. I'm sorry, but you can't wear those boots to school. You need to _____.
   a. follow the dress code   b. win a prize

3. Emily _____ because she was rude to Mr. Moore.
   a. cheated   b. got sent to the principal's office

4. If you're late to class three times in a semester, you will _____.
   a. wear a uniform   b. be assigned to detention

5. Don't use your cell phone during a test. That's _____.
   a. cheating   b. getting extra credit

6. All students must treat each other with respect. We don't tolerate _____ in our school.
   a. bullying   b. being punctual

7. I think you should join the Math Challenge team. You might _____.
   a. win a prize   b. be rude

8. Mike is never late to class. It's important to him to _____.
   a. follow the dress code   b. be punctual

9. A lot of students don't like _____, but I do. It saves me money on clothes.
   a. wearing a uniform   b. being assigned to detention

10. Christine _____ to the Spanish teacher yesterday. Usually, she's very polite.
    a. was assigned to detention   b. was rude

Say it RIGHT!
Notice the way these words are pronounced. Then add one more word for each sound.
/ʊ/ would, could, bullying, _____
/u/ do, rude, you, _____

2. Listen, check, and repeat.

3. Put the phrases from Exercise 1 in the correct categories.

Rewards	Punishments	Good behavior	Bad behavior

Speaking: Actions and consequences

4. **YOUR TURN** Work with a partner. Ask and answer the questions.
   1. What rewards and punishments do students get at your school?
   2. Do you think your school is strict? Why? / Why not?

   Teachers sometimes play a game after we've done good work.

Workbook, p. 36

Reading A School with a Difference; How to Be Safe Online!; Punishment or Rehabilitation?
Conversation Asking for and giving advice
Writing An article about online safety

YOU make the RULES!

A SCHOOL WITH A DIFFERENCE
This week's student reporter, Jodi White, visits the Brooklyn Free School in New York.

It's Wednesday morning, and it's time for the weekly school meeting. This week's topic is "wheels." One student proposes a new rule that students can bring skateboards, skates, and bicycles to school. A teacher suggests that they do this one day a week, and the whole school votes on a "wheels" day for next Friday. As simple as that! Would I be able to change the rules in my school if I wanted to? No, if I wanted to change the rules, it would be really hard!

But the Brooklyn Free School is different. Here the students make the decisions – about everything! They can decide to go to class or they can decide to watch TV or play a computer game, but most students choose to go to class – it's more interesting! When they don't like a class, they just walk out. If I didn't stay until the end of a class at my school, I'd be assigned to detention!

At the Free School, the teachers don't assign students to detention, and no one gets sent to the principal's office. The students choose what they want to study and how. If you were at the school and you wanted to study car mechanics, for example, or cooking, would the school let you do it? Yes. If you wanted to start a new school magazine, you would suggest it, and together the school would find a way to do it.

That's how the Free School works. The ideas come from the students, and everyone works together to make them happen. I'd love to go to the Free School!

DID YOU KNOW...?
There are more than 90 schools like the Brooklyn Free School in the United States. They're sometimes called "anarchistic free schools" or "free skools."

Reading: An article from a school newspaper

1. Look at the title of the article and the name of the school. What kind of school is it? Why do they describe it as "free"?

2. Read and listen to the article about a school in New York. What are two ways that this school is different from your school?

3. Read the article again. Are these sentences true (*T*) or false (*F*)?
   1. The school has meetings every month. ___
   2. The students make suggestions, and the teachers vote on their suggestions. ___
   3. There are no rules. ___
   4. The students choose their own subjects. ___
   5. The teachers don't tell the students what to do. ___
   6. The reporter doesn't want to study at the Free School. ___

4. **YOUR TURN** Work with a partner. Ask and answer the questions.
   1. Would you like to go to a school like the Brooklyn Free School? Why? / Why not?
   2. How much can students change the rules or classes at your school?
   3. What kinds of classes would you like to take that your school doesn't offer? Where could you learn those things outside of school?

> *I think I'd like that school. If you want, you can watch TV!*

> *I'd like it because I could choose what I wanted to study. . . .*

Grammar: Second conditional

5. Complete the chart.

Use the second conditional to describe imaginary situations and possible consequences.	
Imaginary situation	**Possible consequences**
if + simple past **If** I **changed** the school rules,	*would (not)* + base form of the verb students **wouldn't wear** uniforms.
If you **missed** class, **If** she **didn't like** the class,	you _____ **be** assigned to detention. she _____ **go**.
Many American English speakers use *were* rather than *was* after *I, he, she,* and *it,* especially in a more formal style.	
Formal style	**Informal style**
If I _____ rude to my teacher, my parents would be very mad at me.	If I _____ always punctual, I wouldn't be assigned to detention so much.

> Check your answers: Grammar reference, p. 111

6. Circle the correct answers.

1. If I **was** / **would be** rude to a teacher, I **got** / **would be** assigned to detention.
2. If I **didn't** / **wouldn't** pass my finals, my parents **didn't** / **wouldn't** be very happy.
3. If a teacher **sent** / **would send** me to the principal's office, I **felt** / **would feel** embarrassed.
4. My teacher **called** / **would call** my parents if I **didn't** / **wouldn't** go to school.
5. My friends **did** / **would like** to go to the Free School if they **opened** / **would open** one in our town.
6. I **didn't** / **wouldn't** study math if I **went** / **would go** to the Free School.

7. Complete the sentences with the correct form of the verbs.

1. If I _____ (come) home late one night, . . .
   a. my parents _____ (be) very angry. I _____ (get) some kind of punishment.
   b. my parents _____ (talk) to me about the issue.
   c. my parents _____ (not say) anything.
2. If I _____ (say) something rude to my parents, . . .
   a. I _____ (feel) bad, and I _____ (say) sorry immediately.
   b. they _____ (ask) me what I was upset about.
   c. they _____ (punish) me with no TV or computer for a week.
3. If I _____ (borrow) something from my friend without asking, . . .
   a. it _____ (not be) a problem. My friend does it to me all the time!
   b. my friend probably _____ (not talk) to me for a week!
   c. I _____ (put) it back before they noticed.

Second conditional yes/no questions

Use *if* to ask yes/no questions in the second conditional.

If your teacher **got** angry with you in class, **would** you **feel** embarrassed?

Would you **say** anything **if** your teacher **forgot** to give you homework?
Yes, I **would**.
No, I **wouldn't**.

Speaking: If I did that, . . .

8. YOUR TURN Circle the answers in Exercise 7 that are true for you. Then compare your answers with a partner.

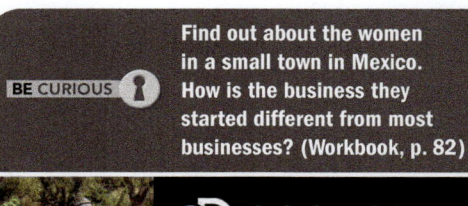

> *If I came home late one night, I'd get some kind of punishment for sure!*

Workbook, p. 37

BE CURIOUS — Find out about the women in a small town in Mexico. How is the business they started different from most businesses? (Workbook, p. 82)

Discovery EDUCATION

6.1 WORKING TOGETHER

Unit 6 | 57

What would YOU DO?

Listening: Would you tell the teacher?

1. Work with a partner. What would you do if you saw one of your classmates cheating on a test? What if you found a wallet full of money in the street?

2. Listen to a conversation between two teenagers, Rachel and Luke. What are they discussing?

3. Listen again. Circle the correct answers.

   1. If Rachel saw a classmate cheating on a test, she would . . .
      a. say nothing and continue with her work.
      b. tell a teacher.
      c. try to cheat as well.

   2. If Luke found a wallet full of money on the street near his school, he would . . .
      a. take it to the nearest police station.
      b. give it to a teacher at school.
      c. keep it.

   3. If Rachel borrowed something from a friend and then lost it, she would . . .
      a. tell her friend.
      b. buy a new one.
      c. say nothing and hope the friend doesn't notice.

Vocabulary: Expressions with *make* and *do*

4. Complete the email with *make* or *do*. Then listen and check your answers.

To: dan@cup.org
From: eric@cup.org
Subject: Advice

Hi Dan,
I need your advice. We have to give presentations in science class tomorrow, and I have a problem. One of my classmates, Jeremy, asked me to ¹ _do_ **him a favor**: He wanted me to help him with his presentation. Jeremy doesn't like science, and he doesn't like to ² _____ **homework**, but I agreed to help him. We started to ³ _____ **research** together, but he was bored. "Let's hurry up so we can ⁴ _____ **something fun**!" he said. He started to copy whole paragraphs from the Internet and paste them into his presentation. I explained that you can use the Internet for research, but you shouldn't copy like that. "It won't ⁵ _____ **a difference**," he said. "Mrs. Lewis won't find out." Then he looked at my presentation and copied from me! I didn't want to ⁶ _____ **him mad**, so I didn't say anything else. I'm new to this school, and I want to ⁷ _____ **friends**, but I also want to ⁸ _____ **the right thing**. What should I do?
Eric

---

5. **YOUR TURN** Work with a partner. Ask and answer the questions.

   1. How often do you do homework with your friends?

   2. Is doing homework with someone a good way to make new friends? Why or why not?

   3. Eric wants to do the right thing. What do you think he should do in this situation?

Grammar: Second conditional Wh- questions

6. Complete the chart.

Use Wh- questions in the second conditional to ask about imaginary situations and possible consequences.

What	would your teacher do	if	one of your classmates _____ on a test?
Who	would you talk to	if	you _____ a serious problem with a friend?
When	would you go to school	if	you _____ the days you went?
If	you wanted to do something fun this weekend,	where	would you _____?
If	you got a new pet,	why	would you _____ one kind of pet over another?

▶ Check your answers: Grammar reference, p. 111

7. Circle the correct answers.

1. What **did / would** you do if you **were / would be** the principal at your school?
2. If you **needed / would need** to find a quiet place to study at your school, where **would you go / did you go**?
3. Who would you **do / did** research on if you **have / had** to give a presentation on someone famous?
4. If you **get / got** perfect grades, what would your parents **say / said**?
5. When would you **apologize / apologized** if you **make / made** your best friend mad – at that moment, or a few days later?
6. If you **have / had** to make a difficult decision, who **will / would** you ask to help you?

8. Complete the conversation.

A: What ¹_____ you _____ (do) if another kid in your school ²_____ (bully) you?
B: I don't know. Maybe I ³_____ (hide).
A: Really? Where ⁴_____ you _____ (hide)?
B: I don't know. But, hiding isn't a good idea. I know! I ⁵_____ (fight) the bully.
A: Really? Where ⁶_____ you _____ (have) the fight?
B: Maybe outside? But, no. A fight ⁷_____ (be) stupid. I ⁸_____ (talk) to someone about the problem.
A: Who ⁹_____ you _____ (tell)?
B: My parents, probably. Let me ask you a question: Why ¹⁰_____ you _____ (ask) me crazy questions like this?
A: It's for the school newspaper. I'm talking to a lot of people about bullying.

> **Get it RIGHT!**
> Use the simple past after *if* with the second conditional.
> *If our teacher **gave** extra credit, my grades would be better.* NOT: ~~If our teacher gives extra credit, my grades would be better.~~

Speaking: In this situation, I would . . .

9. YOUR TURN Work with a partner. Ask and answer the questions.

1. If you were home alone and someone knocked on the door, what would you do?
2. What would you do if you found out your best friend lied to you about lots of things?
3. If you were 18, what would you do that you can't do now?
4. What would you do if you decided to stay home from school one day?

> *If I were home alone and someone knocked on the door, I would make sure I knew the person before I opened the door.*

▶ Workbook, pp. 38–39

REAL TALK 6.2 WHO WOULD YOU TALK TO IF YOU NEEDED ADVICE

I need your ADVICE.

Conversation: I don't know what to do!

1. **REAL TALK** Watch or listen to the teenagers. Check (✓) the three people that are **not** mentioned.

☐ aunt	☐ cousin	☐ mother
☐ best friend	☐ father	☐ neighbor
☐ brother	☐ grandmother	☐ sister

2. **YOUR TURN** Who would you talk to if you needed advice? Tell your partner.

3. Listen to Hayley talking to her friend Josh about a problem. Complete the conversation.

   USEFUL LANGUAGE: Asking for and giving advice
   - If I were you
   - ✓ What's going on?
   - I need some advice.
   - Sure. What's up?
   - What should I do?
   - Have you tried

   Hayley: Josh, can I talk to you?
   Josh: Yes, of course. ¹ _What's going on?_
   Hayley: ² _____ I don't know what to do.
   Josh: ³ _____
   Hayley: Well, there's a girl in my class who is saying nasty things about me.
   Josh: Really? What sort of things?
   Hayley: Oh, that I copy her homework and cheat on tests. It's awful!
   ⁴ _____
   Josh: ⁵ _____, I wouldn't listen to her. What do your other friends say?
   Hayley: They say the same thing. But I can't help it.
   Josh: Hmm. ⁶ _____ talking to her about it?
   Hayley: Yeah, but it doesn't change anything. She keeps doing it.
   Josh: Let's talk to her together. Maybe that will help.
   Hayley: That's a good idea. Thanks, Josh!

4. Practice the conversation with a partner.

5. **YOUR TURN** Work with a partner. Take turns asking for and giving advice. Use the problems below or your own ideas.

   Problem 1
   Someone in your class has taken your backpack. No one knows who took it.

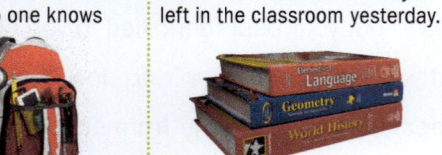

   Problem 2
   You can't find some books you left in the classroom yesterday.

HOW TO BE SAFE ONLINE!

It's easy to bully someone online, and many teenagers suffer from this. So how can you make sure it doesn't happen to you? Follow our essential advice.

> Don't post contact information (address, email, cell phone number) online.
> Check your privacy settings on social networking sites. Make sure you know how to keep your personal information private.
> Don't share your online passwords, not even with your best friends.
> Never respond or retaliate if someone bullies you. This can make things worse.
> You should block any users who send you nasty messages, even if they're your friends.
> Think carefully about posting photos of yourself online. Once your picture is online, anyone can download, share, or even change it.
> Don't ignore cyberbullying or keep it secret. You should ALWAYS tell someone.

Reading to write: An advice article

6. Look at the picture and read the article. What is it about?

◎ Focus on CONTENT
When you write an article to help people solve a problem, you can include this information:
- a title
- the problem you will give advice about
- who the problem affects
- a question that the article will try to answer
- a list of short, clear pieces of advice

7. Read the article again. Does it include all of the things from the Focus on Content box? How many pieces of advice are there?

◎ Focus on LANGUAGE
Giving advice in writing
Use the imperative to give advice in writing.
Affirmative: base form
Block people who are rude to you.
Negative: *Don't* + base form
Don't forget to check your privacy settings.

8. Find one other way to give advice in the article.

9. Complete the sentences.

| ✓ Don't | Make | Never | should | think |

1. *Don't* forward cyberbullying videos or messages about other people.
2. You _____ never give anyone your passwords.
3. If someone bullies you, _____ carefully about changing your user ID and profile.
4. _____ sure you report anything abusive you see online.
5. _____ agree to keep chats with people you don't know "secret."

Writing: An advice article

◯ PLAN
Think of a problem that you think might affect your classmates, friends, or people in your town. Use the guidelines in the Focus on Content box, and make a list of six pieces of advice you would give to solve the problem.

◯ WRITE
Write your article. Use your notes and the online safety article above to help you. Write about 120 words.

◯ CHECK
Can you say "yes" to these questions?
- Is the information from the Focus on Content box in your article?
- Have you given advice using the imperative, both affirmative and negative?

PUNISHMENT OR REHABILITATION?

If a teenager committed a crime in your neighborhood, what do you think should happen?

The case for punishment:
It's all about consequences. If I didn't study for a test, I wouldn't pass it. If I put my hand in a fire, I would be burned. Simple. So if you commit a crime, you should face the consequences, and that's prison. I heard about a program in Switzerland where teenagers who commit crimes get free school, sports, psychological help, and even a place to live. Are you kidding? That's expensive – more expensive than prison. Our tax money should help society, not people who break the rules of society.
Ellie, 15, Portland, Maine

The case for rehabilitation:
What teenagers need when they're in trouble is help – and we need to spend our tax money to help them. The program in Switzerland was expensive, but it helped teenagers stop committing crimes. Teenagers need to learn that there are alternatives to crime. They need to learn skills so that they can get a job. They need to believe that they are valuable members of society. If you throw them in prison and forget about them, they learn to become better criminals, not better citizens.
Collin, 16, Boise, Idaho

? What should we do with teenagers who commit crimes? Lock them up, or help them change their lives?

Culture: Juvenile justice

1. Look at the photo. What do you think society should do with teenagers who commit crimes? Why?

2. Read and listen to the debate. How does Ellie answer the question in Exercise 1? How does Collin answer it?

3. Read the debate again. Answer the questions.
   1. According to Ellie, what should the consequences of committing a crime be?
   2. What did the program in Switzerland give teenagers who committed a crime?
   3. How does Ellie think tax money should be spent?
   4. What does Collin think teenagers in trouble need?
   5. What is the purpose of teaching skills to teenagers who commit a crime?
   6. What does Collin believe happens when you put teenagers in prison?

4. **YOUR TURN** Work with a partner. Ask and answer the questions.
   1. Do you agree with Ellie or Collin? Why?
   2. Is there a program in your country like the program in Switzerland? Do you think it's a good idea?
   3. Can you think of one or two solutions to teenage crime that don't involve prison or expensive programs?

BE CURIOUS Find out about staying safe online. Who does the video say are the number-one victims of identity theft? (Workbook, p. 83)

Discovery EDUCATION
6.3 WATCH YOUR IDENTITY

UNIT 6 REVIEW

Vocabulary

1. Match the words with the definitions.

1. uniform ___
2. detention ___
3. dress code ___
4. punctual ___
5. bullying ___
6. cheating ___

a. on time, not late
b. rules about what clothes to wear
c. copying another student's work
d. special clothes for school
e. a type of punishment
f. being aggressive to another person

Grammar

2. Complete the sentences with the second conditional forms of the verbs.

1. If you _____ (be) more confident, you _____ (make) more friends.
2. If he _____ (not go) to school, he _____ (be) bored.
3. If they _____ (wear) uniforms, they _____ (look) the same.
4. We _____ (have) more free time if we _____ (not have) so much homework.
5. You _____ (not be) so tired if you _____ (not stay) up late.
6. If she _____ (study) harder, she _____ (get) better grades at school.

3. Write questions using the second conditional.

1. What / you / do / if / you / see someone cheating on a test?

   _____

2. Where / you / live / if / you / can go anywhere in the world?

   _____

3. If / you / win / $5,000 / what / you / do?

   _____

4. If / your friend / not answer / your email / what / you / say?

   _____

5. If / you / not pass / your next test / you / feel upset?

   _____

6. What / you / do / if / you / can live forever?

   _____

Useful language

4. Complete the conversation.

going on	I were	What should
Have you	some advice	

Bryce: Hey, Kelly, I really need ¹_____.

Kelly: You do? OK. What's ²_____?

Bryce: I was assigned to detention because I've been late for my history class three times this semester.

Kelly: That's not so terrible.

Bryce: Yes, it is. My parents get really mad about that kind of thing. ³_____ I do?

Kelly: If ⁴_____ you, I would be totally honest and tell them the truth.

Bryce: No, they never listen. They just get mad and stay mad.

Kelly: ⁵_____ tried talking to them? You never know.

Bryce: That's true. I'm not a little kid anymore. Maybe they'll really listen.

Kelly: Give it a try. You never know.

PROGRESS CHECK: Now I can . . .

- ☐ talk about school life.
- ☐ talk about good and bad behavior at school and home.
- ☐ discuss difficult situations.
- ☐ ask for and give advice.
- ☐ write about school rules.
- ☐ discuss different systems for dealing with crime.

7 Smart PLANET

Discovery EDUCATION

BE CURIOUS

- Where Does It All Go?
- What kind of volunteer work do you do?
- Build It Better
- Driving into the Future

1. Describe what you see in this picture.

2. How does this picture make you feel?

3. Which things in the picture are natural and which are man-made?

UNIT CONTENTS

Vocabulary Materials; eco-construction verbs
Grammar Simple present passive; infinitives of purpose; simple past passive
Listening Tour of a museum EcoHouse

Vocabulary: Materials

1. Match the words with the correct pictures.

1. _g_ bricks
2. ___ plastic
3. ___ metal
4. ___ glass
5. ___ water
6. ___ cotton
7. ___ paper
8. ___ cement
9. ___ rubber
10. ___ wood
11. ___ plants

2. Listen, check, and repeat.

3. Write the materials.
   1. We often use this material to make furniture like chairs and tables. _____
   2. This material is very common for making T-shirts. _____
   3. We make tires for cars with this material. _____
   4. We use this material to make books and magazines. _____
   5. We usually use this material to make knives, forks, and spoons. _____
   6. This material is often gray, and we use it to build bridges and buildings. _____

Speaking: What's in your house?

4. **YOUR TURN** Think about your house or apartment. Write as many objects as you can think of for each material below.

Cotton	Glass	Wood	Paper	Rubber	Plastic	Metal

5. Work with a partner. Talk about the things in your house.

   My family has a beautiful glass vase in the living room and . . .

> Workbook, p. 44

Reading Houses Made of Garbage; Volunteers Clean Valley Nature Reserve; Under the Australian Sun
Conversation Apologizing
Writing A newspaper article about an event

Unit 7 | 65

A WAR Against WASTE

HOUSES Made of GARBAGE

Mike Reynolds builds houses from recycled materials. These houses are a symbol of his war against waste. Mike's houses are built using the things that other people throw away. His Earthships (as his houses are called) are beautiful buildings. They are shaped and colored to reflect the landscape around them. He uses bottles to create beautiful walls full of light. There are plants everywhere, inside and out. But the plants and the bottles, like everything else in the Earthships, are not only there for decoration.

Every single material in an Earthship is carefully chosen. Old car tires are used to build strong external walls. The rubber protects the houses from the cold northern winds in winter. These walls are built at the back of the house. The external walls at the front of the house are built from metal cans or glass bottles, instead of bricks. They're held together with earth from the ground around them. No cement is used at all.

The beautiful bottle walls are built to the south to give light during the day. The larger front windows heat the house. They also create perfect conditions for growing all kinds of fruits and vegetables because the plants are protected against the bad weather. When you live in an Earthship, you don't need anything from the outside world. You grow your own food, you get electricity from the sun and wind, and you get water from the rain and snow.

Mike and the Earthship organization use their ability and experience to help people all over the world. In 2010, they visited victims of the earthquake in Haiti. They taught them how to build safe, new homes quickly and cheaply from materials that they could find around them. Mike points out that trash only exists because we humans create it – but we can also learn to recycle it.

DID YOU KNOW...?
Recycled car tires are used to build roads and sidewalks.

Reading: A magazine article

1. **Look at the picture. Work with a partner. Ask and answer the questions.**
   1. What are the people building?
   2. What materials are they using?
   3. Why are they using them?

2. **Read and listen to an article about Mike Reynolds. What kind of houses does he build?**

3. **Read the article again. Answer the questions.**
   1. How does Mike protect his Earthships from the cold?
   2. How does he provide light during the day?
   3. Why does he grow his plants in the front of the house?
   4. How does he get energy and water?
   5. How did he and his organization help other people?
   6. What is Mike's main message to the world?

4. **YOUR TURN Work with a partner. Ask and answer the questions.**
   1. Are the materials that Mike Reynolds uses for his Earthships available where you live? What other recycled materials from your area could be used for an Earthship?
   2. Are Earthships practical or possible where you live?
   3. What is your opinion of Earthships? Would you like to live in an Earthship? What would your ideal Earthship look like?

Grammar: Simple present passive

5. Complete the chart.

Use the passive when it is not important who does the action, or when you don't know who does it. To form the simple present passive, use is/are + past participle.

Active	Passive
Affirmative	
They **make** this wall of bottles.	This wall _____ **made** of bottles.
People **use** car tires to build strong walls.	Car tires **are** _____ to build strong walls.
Negative	
They **don't make** that bottle of plastic.	That bottle **isn't** _____ of plastic.
People **don't build** the houses with bricks.	The houses _____ **built** with bricks.

> Check your answers: Grammar reference, p. 112

6. Complete the sentences with the simple present passive forms of the verbs.

1. The house ___is made___ (make) of bottles and cans.
2. Rubber tires _____ (not recycle) in some areas.
3. The water from the kitchen _____ (reuse) in the yard.
4. The recycling bins _____ (not clean) every week.
5. A lot of energy _____ (consume) in most houses.
6. This wall _____ (not decorate) with colored bottles.

7. Write simple present passive sentences. Use infinitives of purpose.

1. wood / use / build / houses in this neighborhood / .
   Wood is used to build houses in this neighborhood.
2. these plants / grow / provide / people with food / .
   _____
3. walls / design / protect / people from extreme temperatures / .
   _____
4. heat from the sun / use / give / power to the house / .
   _____
5. cans / recycle / create / walls / .
   _____

Infinitives of purpose

Use infinitives of purpose to say why something is done.

*I recycle my bottles **to help the environment**.*

*Plants are used **to prevent flooding**.*

Speaking: Plan a building!

8. YOUR TURN Work with a partner. Plan a new building that is made from recycled materials. What can you do with the materials below? Write your ideas and add other materials and uses. Be creative!

Glass bottles	Car or bike tires	Newspapers	Soda cans	Old clothes
beautiful chandeliers				

9. Join another pair. Tell them about your new building.

> In our building, glass bottles are used to make beautiful chandeliers and lamps.

> And newspapers are used . . .

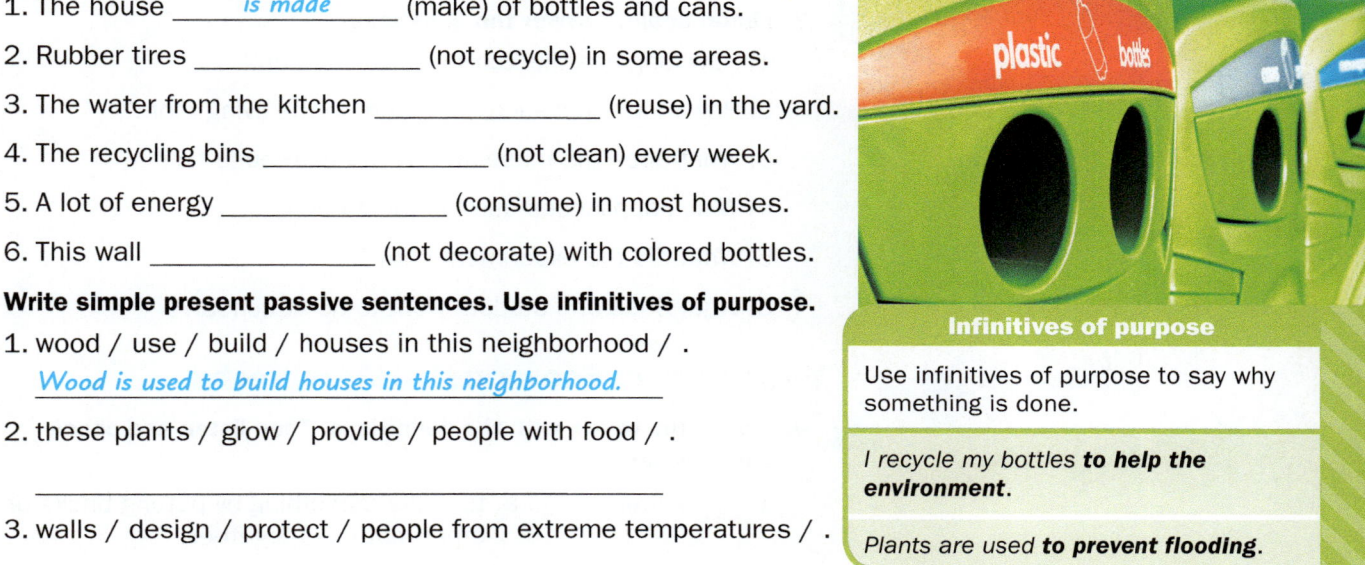

BE CURIOUS Find out about the trash in our oceans. How many kilos of trash do we throw in the oceans every day? (Workbook, p. 84)

Discovery EDUCATION
7.1 WHERE DOES IT ALL GO?

> Workbook, p. 45

New Challenges, NEW SOLUTIONS

Listening: Tour of a museum EcoHouse

1. Look at the picture. How is the room similar to and different from the living room in your home?

2. Listen to a guide explaining the living room. It's part of an exhibit. What kind of living room is it?
   a. A historical living room
   b. A living room of the future
   c. A typical modern living room

3. Listen again. Answer the questions.
   1. How long has the EcoHouse been open?
   2. How many appliances are there in the living room?
   3. What does the museum use the EcoHouse for?
   4. Which appliances use the most energy?
   5. What did the experiment show?
   6. What does one student want to do at school?

Vocabulary: Eco-construction verbs

4. Match the words with the definitions. Then listen and check your answers.

   1. _d_ install
   2. ___ build
   3. ___ design
   4. ___ reduce
   5. ___ discover
   6. ___ change
   7. ___ save
   8. ___ consume

   a. to make something by putting bricks or other materials together
   b. to stop someone or something from being killed or destroyed
   c. to find information, especially for the first time
   d. to put a piece of equipment somewhere and make it ready to use
   e. to use something such as a product, energy, or fuel
   f. to make something less
   g. to make or become different
   h. to draw or plan something, like clothes or buildings

5. **YOUR TURN** Work with a partner. Ask and answer the questions.
   1. What is one thing you could do to reduce trash at school and in your home?
   2. What do you think is going to be important when architects design new buildings in the future?
   3. Are architects the only ones who can discover new building techniques? Who else can participate in the process?

Grammar: Simple past passive

6. Complete the chart.

Use the passive when it is not important who did the action, or when you don't know who did it.
To form the simple past passive, use was/were + past participle.

Active	Passive
Affirmative	
We **built** the EcoHouse in 1985.	The EcoHouse **was built** in 1985.
We **updated** the appliances two months ago.	The appliances _____ **updated** two months ago.
Negative	
We **didn't install** a recycling bin until last year.	A recycling bin **wasn't** _____ until last year.
They **didn't install** solar panels 60 years ago.	Solar panels _____ **installed** 60 years ago.
Use by with the passive to show who did the action.	
The EcoHouse **was designed by** the museum.	
The most energy **was consumed by** the heater.	
Questions and answers with the passive	
When **was** the EcoHouse **built**?	It **was built** in 1985.
_____ the EcoHouse **built** in 1985?	Yes, it **was**.
Were the old apartments **destroyed** this year?	No, they **weren't**.

> Check your answers: Grammar reference, p. 112

7. Complete the paragraph with the simple past passive forms of the verbs.

The building ¹ _was completed_ (complete) in 1985. It ² _____ (build) on a large piece of land outside the city. The air conditioners ³ _____ (install) 10 years ago. They ⁴ _____ (not put) in the bedrooms. The kitchen ⁵ _____ (redesign) two years ago.

8. Rewrite the sentences using the simple past passive and by.

1. The Spanish soccer team won the World Cup for the first time in 2010.
   The World Cup was won by the Spanish soccer team for the first time in 2010.

2. The Chinese found dinosaur bones over 2,000 years ago in Sichuan.
   _____

3. Ray Tomlinson sent the first email in 1971.
   _____

Speaking: Test your knowledge!

9. Put the words in the correct order to make questions.

1. by J. K. Rowling / written / *Romeo and Juliet* / Was / ?
   _____

2. the first *The Hunger Games* movie / was / When / released / ?
   _____

10. YOUR TURN Write four more questions of your own. Use the simple past passive. Then work with a partner. Ask and answer the questions in Exercise 9 and your own questions. Who knows the most answers?

> When was the first cell phone call made?

Get it RIGHT!

Remember to include *was* or *were* in past passive sentences.
The building **was built** in 1985.
NOT: ~~The building built in 1985~~.
People **were taught** to build homes quickly. NOT: ~~People taught to build homes quickly~~.

REAL TALK — 7.2 WHAT KIND OF VOLUNTEER WORK CAN YOU DO IN YOUR SCHOOL OR TOWN?

Be part of the SOLUTION.

Conversation: What kind of volunteer work can you do in your school or town?

1. **REAL TALK** Watch or listen to the teenagers. Which ideas for volunteer work would you like to do? Write 1–6 next to them; 1 is your favorite idea, and 6 is your least favorite idea.

   ___ join after-school clubs
   ___ read to older people
   ___ help older people with their animals
   ___ clean up trash
   ___ babysit
   ___ help in the school garden

2. **YOUR TURN** Do you do volunteer work? What do you do, and why do you do it? If not, why not? Tell your partner.

3. Listen to James talking to Natalie. Complete the conversation.

USEFUL LANGUAGE: Apologizing

| I didn't mean to | I'm really sorry. | It was my fault. | ✓ My apologies. |

James: Hey, Natalie. What happened to you yesterday?
Natalie: Yesterday? What do you mean?
James: Don't you remember? We agreed to go to the park and clean up trash? A whole bunch of us were there. You said you wanted to do it.
Natalie: Oh, no! [1] *My apologies.* I forgot about that.
James: Natalie, I sent you a text to remind you!
Natalie: I know. [2] _____ I didn't set my alarm clock.
James: You were supposed to bring trash bags. We were counting on you.
Natalie: [3] _____ What did you do?
James: I had to call my dad and ask him to bring us trash bags. He was pretty mad because he was busy with something else.
Natalie: [4] _____ forget. I feel really bad about that.
James: It's OK. We're doing it again next month. Can we count on you?
Natalie: Yes! I'll be there. I promise.

4. Practice the conversation with a partner.

5. **YOUR TURN** Work with a partner. Take turns apologizing to a friend and explaining what the problem was. Use the situations below.

Situation A
You forgot to help your friend read books to children at a library. Your friend had to do it alone.

Situation B
You didn't help your friend prepare a presentation for class about recycling. Your friend was up really late working on it.

Say it RIGHT!

To make adjectives stronger, you can use words like *really*, *very*, and *extremely*. Put extra stress on these words. Listen and repeat the sentences.

I'm **really** sorry.
They were **very** noisy.
We're **extremely** excited!

Volunteers Clean Valley Nature Reserve by Chris Davies

Last Sunday, about 100 people went to the Valley Nature Reserve to clean up the river. The event was organized by the Valley Conservation Society, which helps to protect the environment. Every year, local volunteers clean up trash that is thrown in the river. This year, I was one of them. We picked up hundreds of plastic bottles, plastic bags, and metal cans. That stuff was disgusting! The Society also removes non-native plants from the land near the river. These plants kill off native species and affect biodiversity. At the Valley Nature Reserve, we cut down kudzu, a pretty, but dangerous, plant. The cleanup was hard work, but it was fun. And the river looked great! Why not join us next time? We're already planning next year's event. It'll be in April. For more information, go to the Valley Nature Reserve website. ■

Reading to write: Cleaning up a river

6. Look at the photo. What kind of trash did the volunteers find? Read the article and check.

> ### Focus on CONTENT
> When you write a newspaper article, ask yourself these questions before you begin:
> - What was the event?
> - When was it?
> - Where was it?
> - Who was involved?
> - What did they do?
> - What were the results?
> - What will happen next?

7. Underline the answers to the Focus on Context box questions in the article.

> ### Focus on LANGUAGE
> Don't repeat the same word or words too much when you write. Use different words to refer to something you wrote about before.
> *The event* = the Valley Nature Reserve cleanup
> *I was one of them* = one of the volunteers

8. Write what the words from the article refer to.
    1. *These plants* kill off native species: <u>non-native plants</u>
    2. *That stuff* was disgusting: _____
    3. . . . but *it* was fun: _____
    4. *It*'ll be in April: _____
    5. *a pretty but dangerous plant*: _____

Writing: A newspaper article about an event

☐ **PLAN**
Plan your newspaper article about an event. Use the list in the Focus on Content box and make notes.

☐ **WRITE**
Write your article. Use your notes to help you. Write about 120 words.

☐ **CHECK**
Can you say "yes" to these questions?
- Is the information from the Focus on Content box in your article?
- Did you answer the questions from the Focus on Content box?

Workbook, pp. 48–49

UNDER THE
AUSTRALIAN SUN

Australia is one of the sunniest countries on the planet, and sun is an important part of Australia's traditional outdoor lifestyle. Barbecues are held in sunny backyards 12 months a year. People spend days on end surfing at beautiful golden beaches. One in four homes has a swimming pool in the yard. You don't believe me? Look out the airplane window when you land at Sydney Airport. But there's more to sun than fun!

Australia gets more than 3,500 hours of sunlight a year – that's 10 hours a day – and solar energy is big business. Australia has invested enormously in solar energy. Solar panels provide energy to houses, schools, businesses, and factories all over the country. They have reduced the country's energy bills and had a very positive environmental impact.

However, there's a price to pay for so much sunshine. Rays from the sun can be very dangerous. The risk of skin cancer is high, so ads everywhere tell people to *Slip! Slop! Slap!* This very successful three-step approach was invented by experts to remind us what to use to protect our skin.

- First, *slip* on some special clothing. Clothes with special sun filters were invented by Australians and are really popular.
- Next, *slop* on some powerful sunscreen – even if you're only going out for 10 minutes. Use sunscreens with a sun protection factor (SPF) of at least 30+.
- Finally, *slap* on a big hat. Find a big hat that is designed so the sun doesn't hit your head or neck.

So remember, it's great to have fun in the sun, but wherever you are, and whatever you're doing – having a barbecue, chilling out at the pool, or surfing at the beach – don't forget to SLIP, SLOP, **SLAP!**

Culture: Good sunshine, bad sunshine

1. Look at photos *a* and *b*. What can you see in each photo? What connects the two photos?
2. Read and listen to the article. Is the Australian attitude toward the sun mainly positive or mainly negative?
3. Read the article again. Answer the questions.
   1. How does the sun influence the Australian way of life?
   2. Why are solar panels successful in Australia?
   3. Why is the sun a problem in Australia?
   4. What are the three things you should slip on, slop on, and slap on?
4. **YOUR TURN** Work with a partner. Ask and answer the questions.
   1. Would you like to visit Australia? Why? / Why not?
   2. What's the sunniest place in your country?
   3. Is solar energy common in your country?
   4. How do you protect yourself from the sun?

DID YOU KNOW...?
Eighty percent of Australians live within 50 kilometers of the coast.

BE CURIOUS Find out about a natural disaster in a town in Kansas, in the United States. How was the town different after it was rebuilt? (Workbook, p. 85)

Discovery EDUCATION
7.3 BUILD IT BETTER

UNIT 7 REVIEW

Vocabulary

1. Write the name of each material.

1. G L A S S
2. B _ _ _ _ _
3. W _ _ _ _
4. P _ _ _ _ _ _
5. P _ _ _ _ _
6. M _ _ _ _

Grammar

2. Rewrite the sentences. Use the simple present passive.

1. They recycle these metal cans.
   These metal cans are recycled.

2. They make these sweaters from plastic bottles.
   _____

3. They use corn to make heating oil.
   _____

4. They produce electricity from this water.
   _____

5. They build these houses from organic materials.
   _____

3. Complete the questions and answers with the simple past passive forms of the verbs.

build	discover	✓ make
destroy	grow	

1. When __was__ the first talking movie __made__?
   It __was made__ in 1927.

2. When _____ tea first _____ in China?
   Tea _____ 4,000 years ago.

3. Where _____ gold _____ in the 1800s?
   Gold _____ in California in the 1800s.

4. When _____ Pompeii _____ by a volcanic eruption?
   Pompeii _____ by a volcanic eruption in 79 CE.

5. Where _____ the first public railways _____?
   The first public railways _____ in England in the 1800s.

Useful language

4. Complete the conversation.

really sorry	I didn't mean to	apologies	was my fault

Mom: Kevin, don't throw out the soda cans and newspapers with the trash! We recycle those.

Kevin: Oh, yeah. I'm [1]_____. I totally forgot.

Mom: But we talked about this last month. Everyone in the house was going to help recycle. Remember?

Kevin: Yeah. My [2]_____. I'll try to do better.

Mom: Thank you. Also, you have to clean the kitchen after you make snacks. Last night, it was a mess!

Kevin: Yeah, that [3]_____. I made a snack and then went to bed. I was too tired to clean it up.

Mom: Kevin, come on.

Kevin: Sorry, Mom. [4]_____ make you mad. It won't happen again.

PROGRESS CHECK: Now I can . . .

- ☐ identify materials.
- ☐ talk about how people recycle and reuse materials.
- ☐ talk about eco-construction.
- ☐ apologize.
- ☐ write a newspaper article.
- ☐ discuss solar energy and sun safety.

CLIL PROJECT

7.4 DRIVING INTO THE FUTURE, p. 119

8 Run for Cover!

Discovery EDUCATION

BE CURIOUS

- Land of Volcanoes
- Do you often lose things?
- Storm Chasers

1. Describe what you see in this picture.

2. Tornadoes sometimes appear in movies or TV shows. Have you ever seen a tornado on screen? What was happening?

3. Have you ever seen a tornado in real life? How would you react if you did?

UNIT CONTENTS

Vocabulary Natural disasters; survival essentials
Grammar Past perfect; past perfect *yes/no* questions; past perfect and simple past
Listening Survival story

Vocabulary: Natural disasters

1. Match the words with the correct pictures.

1. _b_ tsunami
2. ___ volcanic eruption
3. ___ earthquake
4. ___ flood
5. ___ forest fire
6. ___ tornado
7. ___ hurricane
8. ___ landslide
9. ___ avalanche

2. Listen, check, and repeat.

3. Match the news reports with disasters (a–i) from Exercise 1.
1. "The wave is enormous. It's like a wall of water." ___
2. "The mountain is very dangerous. Rocks can fall at any time." ___
3. "The flames are now covering the hills, but people's homes are not in danger." ___
4. "The building is shaking. It's really frightening." ___
5. "I can see smoke and hot lava coming down the mountain." ___
6. "The funnel of wind pulled the roof off of a house, and it landed three kilometers away." ___

Say it RIGHT!
Pay attention to the pronunciation of these vowel sounds:
/æ/ dis**a**ster, l**a**ndslide, n**a**tural
/ɒ/ r**o**ck, imp**o**ssible, n**o**t
Find one more example of each sound in Exercise 3.
_____ _____

Speaking: Terror or excitement?

4. YOUR TURN Work with a partner. Ask and answer the questions.
1. Which of the disasters from Exercise 1 are possible in your country?
2. What's the worst type of natural disaster, in your opinion? Why?
3. Do you know anyone who's experienced any of these disasters?
4. What's one more natural disaster not listed here?

> Where we live, lots of these natural disasters are possible: earthquakes, floods, hurricanes, and landslides.

▶ Workbook, p. 50

Reading Krakatoa; Story Source; Chasing the Storms
Conversation Asking about and talking about personal problems
Writing A story about a personal experience

Unit 8 | 75

The Loudest Sound in MODERN HISTORY

KRAKATOA

What's the loudest noise you can imagine? Double it and that might be close to the noise that the volcanoes on Krakatoa island made when they erupted in 1883. Scientific experts say that it was the loudest sound in modern history. People heard it in Australia, more than 3,000 kilometers away.

Krakatoa is a volcanic island between the islands of Java and Sumatra in Indonesia. When the volcanoes erupted, the explosions created a tsunami with waves more than 40 meters high. In fact, the tsunami caused more deaths than the volcanoes themselves. It killed 34,000 people and destroyed 165 towns and villages.

A huge cloud of dust traveled around the planet. As a result, the temperature of the world dropped one degree. The weather didn't return to normal until five years later, in 1888. People who saw the event said that the cloud had caused fantastic colors in the sky.

Terrible eruptions continued for weeks. Any survivors on other islands who hadn't escaped yet found out that they couldn't escape. They watched the explosions from a distance and organized festivals to celebrate the volcano. What had caused the eruptions? They didn't know. They also didn't know that the eruptions were so serious.

The Krakatoa volcano didn't erupt again until 1927. This eruption created a new island at the same location. There were more eruptions between 2009 and 2012, but they weren't dangerous.

Today, Indonesia has 130 active volcanoes – more than any other country in the world. So a new eruption is possible at any time!

Reading: A magazine article

1. **Look at the title and the picture. What do you think the article is about?**

2. **Read and listen to the article. What was the loudest sound in history?**

3. **Read the article again. Are the sentences true (T) or false (F)?**
   1. The volcanoes on Krakatoa island erupted in 1883. ___
   2. More people died because of the tsunami than the volcanic eruptions. ___
   3. After the volcanic eruptions, the weather quickly returned to normal. ___
   4. People living on nearby islands knew exactly what caused the eruptions. ___
   5. Krakatoa had several dangerous eruptions between 2009 and 2012. ___
   6. No other countries have as many volcanoes as Indonesia. ___

4. **YOUR TURN Work with a partner. Ask and answer the questions.**
   1. Why do you think there were climatic differences for five years after the volcano?
   2. Are there any areas with volcanoes in or near your country? Where are they? Are they still active?
   3. Have you heard about any recent volcanic eruptions or tsunamis? What do you remember about them?

DID YOU KNOW...?
There are over 500 active volcanoes in the world. A large horseshoe-shaped area around the Pacific Ocean is called the "Ring of Fire." Over half the world's active volcanoes can be found there.

Grammar: Past perfect

5. Complete the chart.

Use the past perfect to refer to something that happened before a specific time in the past. To form the past perfect, use had + past participle.	
Affirmative	**Negative**
I was interested in Krakatoa because I **had read** a book about it.	I just read about Krakatoa. I **hadn't heard** about it before then.
The volcano _____ **been** fairly quiet for several years before the eruption.	I visited Indonesia last year. I _____ **been** there before, so it was new to me.
What _____ you **heard** about volcanoes before you visited one? Why _____ **n't** you **researched** anything about Indonesia before you went there?	
Contractions had = 'd had not = **hadn't**	

> Check your answers: Grammar reference, p. 113

6. Complete the sentences with the past perfect forms of the verbs.

1. I _____ (read) about the volcanic eruption at Pompeii, but I didn't know much about Krakatoa.

2. Alan was surprised when he heard the thunder. When _____ the storm _____ (begin)?

3. We _____ (not have) an earthquake before 2004. Since then, we've had three!

4. There were two floods in our town last summer. Before that, I _____ (see) only one flood in 10 years.

5. Sadie went to Europe for the first time last summer. She _____ (not be) there before that.

6. I heard students laughing, and then I heard a loud noise. What _____ they _____ (do)?

7. Put the words in the correct order to make questions.

1. you / about Krakatoa / heard / today / before / had

   Had you heard about Krakatoa before today?

2. before the day of the show / had / bought the tickets / he

   _____

3. her teacher / Julie / had / met / before class started

   _____

4. had / before your parents came home / cleaned / you / your room

   _____

Past perfect yes/no questions	
Had you ever **seen** a tornado before you moved here?	Yes, I **had**. / No, I **hadn't**.
Had Amber **known** about the volcano on the next island?	Yes, she **had**. / No, she **hadn't**.

Speaking: Before the disaster, . . .

8. Imagine a volcano erupted 30 kilometers from your home. You and your family survived because you were prepared. Write three things you had done to prepare for the disaster.

1. *Before the eruption, I had bought extra water.*
2. _____
3. _____

BE CURIOUS — Find out about volcanoes in Russia. What is Sasha's job? (Workbook, p. 86)

Discovery EDUCATION — 8.1 LAND OF VOLCANOES

9. YOUR TURN Work in pairs. Talk about your preparations. Who was better prepared?

> Before the eruption, I had bought extra water.

> That's good. I had forgotten that. But I had asked my mother to fill the gas tank of the car.

Workbook, p. 51

Unit 8 | 77

Survival by ALL MEANS!

Listening: Survival story

1. Work with a partner. Ask and answer the questions.

1. Do you enjoy exercising outdoors or walking in nature? Where have you done that and what was it like?
2. What kinds of things would you take with you if you were on a long hike or walking a long distance?

2. Listen to two friends discussing a news story about a hiker. Is it a happy or a sad story?

3. Listen again. Answer the questions.

1. What's the climate in Queensland like?
   _____
2. What happened when the hiker was out running?
   _____
3. What was the weather like?
   _____
4. What had Sam brought with him?
   a bottle of _____, _____, _____, packs of _____
5. How did the contact lenses save him?
   _____
6. How did they find him in the end?
   _____
7. How long was he lost?
   _____

Vocabulary: Survival essentials

4. Match the words and phrases with the correct pictures. Then listen and check your answers.

1. ___ sunscreen
2. ___ water bottle
3. ___ sunglasses
4. ___ compass
5. ___ map
6. ___ sleeping bag
7. ___ penknife
8. ___ flashlight
9. ___ first-aid kit

5. YOUR TURN Work with a partner. What's the most important survival equipment if you get lost in the following situations? Give reasons.

a. In the mountains in the winter
b. In a forest at night
c. In the middle of a city

Grammar: Past perfect and simple past

6. Read the sentences. Then circle the correct answer to complete the rules.

> The young man's parents **called** the police after he **had been** gone for three days.
> The boy **had drunk** the liquid from all the contact lens cases when they **found** him.
> The boy **didn't tell** his story until he **had drunk** a lot of water.
>
> 1. We **can / can't** use the past perfect and the simple past in the same sentence.
> 2. We use the **simple past / past perfect** for the action that was completed first.

> Check your answers: Grammar reference, p. 113

7. Circle the correct answers.

1. Kent _____ about the weather until he _____ outside for a few minutes.
   a. didn't think / had been   b. had thought / had been
2. After Jen _____ her map for a long time, she _____ to turn left.
   a. studied / had decided   b. had studied / decided
3. The skier's family _____ worried only after the avalanche _____.
   a. had gotten / had happened   b. got / had happened
4. By the time my father _____, I _____ the party.
   a. had called / left   b. called / had left

8. Complete the text with the simple past or past perfect forms of the verbs. Then listen and check your answers.

I ¹_____saw_____ (see) an interesting movie last night. It was the true story of a guy named Aron Ralston. He was alone in a canyon in a national park. A large rock ²_____ (fall) on his right hand, and his hand was stuck between the rock and a wall. Unfortunately, before he ³_____ (leave) home, he ⁴_____ (not tell) his friends or family where he was going. They didn't know he was lost. He was in the canyon for five days. He ⁵_____ (drink) all his water already, and he ⁶_____ (eat) all his food, when he had an idea. He ⁷_____ (bring) along a small, cheap penknife, so he ⁸_____ (use) it to cut off his arm. It was terrible, but he did it. He was free. He started walking and found a family in the park. After they ⁹_____ (give) him some water, they ¹⁰_____ (call) emergency services. He survived! It was a very exciting story.

> **Get it RIGHT!**
> Use the past perfect, not the present perfect, for referring to events completed before another past moment.
> After I **had read** three books about forest fires, I decided to become a firefighter. NOT: ~~After I have read three books about forest fires, I decided to become a firefighter.~~

Speaking: I hadn't done my homework yet!

9. Think about what you did yesterday. Write down one thing you had done, and one thing you hadn't done, by the time you did each thing in the box.

| had breakfast | ate lunch | went to bed |
| got to school | had dinner | |

By the time I had breakfast, I had taken a shower.

10. YOUR TURN Work with a partner. Ask and answer questions about the things you did.

> Had you taken a shower by the time you had breakfast?
>
> Yes, I had. What about you?
>
> No, I hadn't. But I had made my bed.

Workbook, pp. 52–53

REAL TALK 8.2 DO YOU OFTEN LOSE THINGS?

Don't PANIC!

Conversation: Do you often lose things?

1. **REAL TALK** Watch or listen to the teenagers. Check (✓) the things that are mentioned.

   ☐ cell phone ☐ sunglasses ☐ bike
   ☐ pencil ☐ remote control ☐ keys

2. **YOUR TURN** Do you often lose things? Tell your partner about things you have lost, what happened, and how you felt.

3. Listen to Adam and Daniela talking about a problem. Complete the conversation.

USEFUL LANGUAGE: Asking about and talking about personal problems

I don't know what to do! ✓ What's the matter? Don't panic! Oh, no! Let me think.

Adam: Hi, Daniela! ¹ _What's the matter?_
Daniela: I can't find my backpack! It has all my books in it!
Adam: ² _____ When did you last see it?
Daniela: I remember I put it in my locker before gym class.
Adam: Did you get it after gym?
Daniela: I don't remember. I went to the varsity basketball game right after that.
Adam: Did you have it at the game?
Daniela: I don't know. Maybe. I went to the mall with Emily. The game had finished, and we were hungry. And then we went to the park.
Adam: Did you leave it in the park?
Daniela: I'm not sure. I know Emily remembered her backpack. I asked her where she had bought it. But then I came home and when I realized I didn't have it, I went back. It wasn't there!
Adam: OK. ³ _____ Maybe you left it in the mall, in one of the stores.
Daniela: No, I don't think so. For one thing, no one has called me.
Adam: Had you written your name or phone number on your backpack?
Daniela: Yes. Now what? ⁴ _____
Adam: OK, hang on. ⁵ _____ OK, I have an idea. Let's go to the park and see if it's there. Then we'll go to the mall and ask for it at the Lost and Found. Then we'll go to school. Who knows? Maybe you left it in class.

4. Practice the conversation with a partner.

5. **YOUR TURN** Work with a partner. Describe a personal problem. Have your partner try to help you.

Problem 1	Problem 2
You're at school. Your cell phone isn't in your bag. It's new, and it was expensive. It has all your friends' phone numbers in it and hundreds of pictures and songs. You had it this morning at home.	You're at a friend's house. You can't find your flash drive. It has all the work you did for a group presentation on it. You need it tomorrow. You had it earlier today at school.

| Home | **STORIES** | Music | Movies |

STORY SOURCE
Do you have a scary or difficult story to tell? Did you have a scary or difficult experience? Write and tell us what happened.

One afternoon last April, I was at home. I had turned the TV on and was about to watch my favorite show when suddenly, the electricity went off. Then my mom called to say that a tornado was in the area. Where I live, there are tornadoes every year, so, naturally, we had learned what to do at school.

We went down to the basement and hid in a closet. We could hear the storm, louder and louder, and then the walls started to shake. I had been a little scared the time before, but this time I was terrified. After about three minutes, when everything had become quiet again, we went to the kitchen to look outside. I saw that our house was OK, but unfortunately, the house next door was destroyed.

I called my mom immediately. My parents were safe, too. It was a horrible experience, but fortunately, we all survived.

Reading to write: A blog about an experience

6. Look at the picture. What experience is the writer describing? What do you think your reaction to this experience would be?

Focus on CONTENT
When you write about an experience, you can include this information:
- When it happened
- Where you were
- What happened
- How you felt
- The end of the story

7. Read the blog again. Underline the five pieces of information from the Focus on Content box.

Focus on LANGUAGE
Adverbs
Use adverbs to link ideas together and make the story more dramatic and interesting.
. . . when **suddenly**, the electricity went off.

8. Find four more examples of adverbs in the blog.

suddenly _____   _____   _____   _____

9. Complete the sentences with the adverbs in Exercise 8.

1. I had always lived in a place where there were hurricanes, so ___naturally___ I knew what to do when we heard the warning.

2. We didn't wait for the authorities to tell us to leave when the floods started. We left _____.

3. The earthquake was strong, but _____, there was no tsunami afterwards.

4. _____ for our neighbors, the forest fire burned part of their house. It was ruined.

5. Jeff was sleeping when _____, he heard a loud noise.

Writing: A story about a personal experience

PLAN
Plan your personal story for a website. Use the list in the Focus on Content box and make notes.

WRITE
Write your story for the website. Use your notes and the blog to help you. Write about 120 words.

CHECK
Can you say "yes" to these questions?
- Did you include the information from the Focus on Content box?
- Did you use adverbs like *suddenly* to make the writing more dramatic?

CHASING THE STORMS

Tornadoes bring heavy rain and terrible winds – the strongest tornadoes travel at 400 kilometers per hour and are 80 kilometers wide. They are very destructive. Storm chasers are people who follow the tornadoes and try to get as close as possible. Today's interview is with Todd Robson, a storm chaser in Tornado Alley.

What is Tornado Alley?
It's the large area in the middle of the United States. It goes from Iowa in the north to Louisiana in the south. Most of the world's tornadoes happen in Tornado Alley. Every year, there are 1,000 or more tornadoes here!

Why are there so many tornadoes in Tornado Alley?
The summers are really hot, and there are lots of thunderstorms. Those are favorable conditions for tornadoes. Most tornadoes in Tornado Alley happen between March and August, but they can happen at any time of the year.

What's it like living in Tornado Alley?
New buildings in Tornado Alley have to have strong roofs and good foundations. A lot of people have special shelters underground – storm cellars – that protect them from tornadoes. And most neighborhoods have loud tornado sirens that warn them that a tornado is nearby.

Why are you a storm chaser?
Well, it's really exciting, but it isn't just a hobby. It's my job, too. Scientists need to understand storms better so that we can predict when they're coming and warn people.

I've read about storm-chasing tours. Do they really exist?
Yes! People can pay to go on storm-chasing trips. It's scary, and it can be a bit dangerous, but it's fun. Most of our tours are from April to June, and we drive all over Tornado Alley looking for storms. It's incredible!

Culture: Tornado Alley

1. Look at the photo. What kind of extreme weather do you see? What do you think the people in the car are doing?

2. Read and listen to the interview. Check your answers in Exercise 1.

3. Read the interview again. Complete the summary.

   Todd Robson is a storm chaser in ¹_____. Tornadoes bring strong winds and ²_____. They can travel at ³_____. There are more than ⁴_____ tornadoes in Tornado Alley each year, where the summers are ⁵_____ and there are lots of thunderstorms. Many people have ⁶_____ that protect them from tornadoes. Some people chase storms because it's exciting, but scientists want to understand them better to ⁷_____ when they're coming. If you want to chase storms, the best time to do it is from ⁸_____ to June.

4. **YOUR TURN** Work with a partner. Ask and answer the questions.
   1. Why do you think people want to watch storms?
   2. Do you know anyone who's afraid of storms?
   3. Would you like to go on a storm-chasing tour? Why? / Why not?

DID YOU KNOW…?

If you're near a tornado, the safest place is underground – in the basement of a house or in a special shelter.

BE CURIOUS Find out about some scientists who study tornadoes. What is an F5 tornado? (Workbook, p. 87)

8.3 STORM CHASERS

UNIT 8 REVIEW

Vocabulary

1. Match the words with the definitions.

1. ___ earthquake
2. ___ avalanche
3. ___ hurricane
4. ___ eruption
5. ___ flood

a. powerful movements below the Earth's surface
b. an explosion inside a volcano
c. very strong winds that can cause a lot of damage
d. a large quantity of water that suddenly covers land and houses
e. a large quantity of ice or snow falling down a mountain

Grammar

2. Complete the paragraph with the past perfect forms of the verbs.

| notice | read | see | ski | start | ✓ travel |

Last year, I was skiing in Utah with my family. We ¹ _had traveled_ to Utah before, but this was our first visit to this ski resort. My sister and I ² _____ avalanche warning signs in other areas, but there were no signs where we were that day. We ³ _____ down the hill, and a minute later, I heard a loud sound. I ⁴ _____ in a book that avalanches were loud, but this sounded like a train. A loud train! Suddenly, I saw a huge wall of snow coming down the hill after us. I shouted at my sister to ski fast and to follow me. We ⁵ _____ most of the way down the hill, as fast as we could go, when the avalanche reached us. We were covered in snow and couldn't find a way to escape. Luckily, some people ⁶ _____ us, and they had called a rescue crew.

3. Complete the sentences and questions with the past perfect or simple present forms of the verbs.

1. I _didn't see_ (not see) sharks until I _had left_ (leave) the ocean.
2. After we _____ (be) hiking for three hours, it _____ (start) raining.
3. The hikers _____ (not see) the landslide warning signs before they _____ (begin) walking down the hill.
4. The emergency workers _____ (not stop) looking for survivors until they _____ (make) sure everyone was safe.
5. She _____ (not drink) all the water in her bottle, so she _____ (share) some of it with her friend.
6. We _____ (feel) terrible when we saw all the houses the hurricane _____ (destroy).

Useful language

4. Complete the conversation.

| don't | Let me | Oh | ✓ What's the | what to do |

Maria: Kate! Wake up! Look at that!
Kate: What? ¹ _What's the_ matter?
Maria: There's a spider in our tent. A big one. Look over there!
Kate: ² _____, no! Now what?
Maria: I don't know ³ _____! Do you?
Kate: Well, first of all, ⁴ _____ panic.
Maria: I'm trying not to. But look at it. It's huge!
Kate: I know. OK. Hang on. ⁵ _____ think.
Maria: Let's cover it with a towel and throw it outside.
Kate: Good idea. Get your towel.
Maria: My towel? Are you serious? Get your towel.
Kate: Maria, any towel is OK. Let's get going!

PROGRESS CHECK: Now I can . . .

☐ discuss natural disasters.
☐ ask and answer questions about past experiences.
☐ discuss past events.
☐ ask about and discuss personal problems.
☐ write about a difficult past experience.
☐ discuss tornadoes and people who chase tornadoes.

9 He SAID, She SAID

Discovery EDUCATION

BE CURIOUS

- Social Networks
- What do you think about celebrity gossip? 
- The Language of the Future? 
- Pictures with Meaning 

1. Describe what you see in this picture.

2. What kinds of things do you and your friends like to talk about?

3. When you're not together, how do you communicate with your friends?

UNIT CONTENTS

Vocabulary Reporting verbs; Communication methods
Grammar Quoted speech vs. reported speech; reported questions
Listening Short conversations

Vocabulary: Reporting verbs

1. Match the words with the definitions.

1. _e_ say
2. ___ explain
3. ___ remind
4. ___ whisper
5. ___ tell
6. ___ shout
7. ___ announce
8. ___ promise
9. ___ suggest
10. ___ complain

a. to speak very quietly (7 letters)
b. to express an idea for someone to consider (7 letters)
c. to say something very loudly (5 letters)
d. to make someone remember something (6 letters)
e. to tell someone about a fact, thought, or opinion (3 letters)
f. to say you're unhappy or don't like something (8 letters)
g. to say you will certainly do something (7 letters)
h. to make something easy to understand (7 letters)
i. to share news, stories, or information with someone (4 letters)
j. to say something officially (8 letters)

2. Listen, check, and repeat.

3. Complete the sentences with words from Exercise 1.

1. I usually forget to clean my room on Saturdays. My mother has to _remind_ me.
2. My brother's action figure was broken when he bought it. My father went to the store to _____, and he got his money back.
3. After my baby sister finally fell asleep, my mother asked us to _____ so we wouldn't wake her up.
4. I love it when my grandmother comes over. She likes to _____ me stories from when she was little.
5. Mr. Black is a great teacher. He can _____ really hard concepts so that we can understand them.
6. Jessica usually stays out too late, but this time she _____ her parents she would be home on time.

Speaking: Tell about a time when you . . .

4. YOUR TURN Work with a partner. Ask and answer the questions.

1. When was the last time you shouted? Where were you, and why did you shout?
2. Do you know someone who complains a lot? Who? Do you usually agree with this person?
3. When was the last time you promised to do something? Did you do it? Why? / Why not?

> Once, when I was younger, I promised to make dinner with my little sister. We made dinner, but it was terrible!

Say it RIGHT!

When a word ends in the final consonants *d*, *l*, *m*, and *n*, put your tongue in the position to say that letter, but don't say it. Native speakers put more emphasis on the vowel. Practice these sentences:
*I don't understan**d**. Can you please explai**n**?*
*There's nothing to te**ll**. He didn't come ho**m**e.*

Workbook, p. 58

Reading Communication Changes; Are Cell Phones Good for Teenagers?; The World Speaks One Language
Conversation Comparing different accounts of a story
Writing An essay about social networking sites

The Reality of COMMUNICATION TODAY

COMMUNICATION CHANGES
by Amanda Mitchell

Teenagers love their cell phones and social networking sites, but there's conflict at home because of it. I talked to kids, parents, and experts to find out what's going on.

1. ___ "My cell phone is a great way for me to communicate with my friends," student Sarah Davis says. Sarah explained that she wanted to hang out with her friends after school – at the mall or in the park – but these days it wasn't easy. She said her mother, Becky, worried about her going out alone. "So, we go to social networking sites and hang out together that way." Becky isn't happy about it. "That's all she does," she complains.

2. ___ In the past 30 years, parents have become more concerned about security issues. Becky explained that kids in her generation hung out together every day. They rode their bikes to the mall, to each other's houses, or to the park. "But I just don't think that's safe anymore," she says.

3. ___ Psychologist Dr. Richard Turner said that conflict about cell phone use is becoming a common problem in families. "These kids grew up with cell phones. At the same time, parents are uncomfortable with the constant cell phone use. Obviously, families need to find a balance between safety concerns and a teenager's need to be with friends."

4. ___ Students are busier than they used to be. This is another reason why they spend time on social networking sites. "Universities like students who are active and engaged," student Mike Owens explains. That means that Mike does sports or other activities every day after school. "There's just no time to hang out with my friends. We use social networking sites instead," Mike laughs. He said that his parents sometimes get upset about this. "But what can I do? It's the reality!"

DID YOU KNOW…?
The first handheld cell phones were used as car phones. They cost $4,000 to $9,000 in today's money and were so big and heavy that people called them "The Brick."

Reading: A magazine article

1. Read the possible paragraph headings for an article. What do you think the article is about?

a. Conflict in families
b. Then and now
c. No free time
d. A great way to communicate

2. Read and listen to the article. Match the headings (a–d) in Exercise 1 with the paragraphs. *(9.03)*

3. Read the possible paragraph headings for an article again. Answer the questions.

1. Why isn't it easy for Sarah to hang out with her friends at the mall?
2. Why does Becky complain about Sarah's cell phone use?
3. Where did Becky and her friends hang out 30 years ago?
4. What does Dr. Turner say is becoming a source of conflict in many families?
5. What kind of students do universities look for?
6. What does Mike do after school?

4. YOUR TURN Work with a partner. Ask and answer the questions.

1. Where's your favorite place to hang out with your friends?
2. What social networking sites do you use most? Why?
3. What do you imagine social networking sites will be like in 10 years?

Grammar: Quoted speech vs. reported speech

5. Complete the chart with the words in the box.

| can | Future with *will* | Present perfect | Simple past | ✓ Simple present |

Use reported speech to tell others what another person said.

		Quoted speech	Reported speech
1.	Simple present	"It **isn't** right," she said.	She said that it **wasn't** right.
2.	_____	"We **spent** the whole day together," she told me.	She told me that they **had spent** the whole day together.
3.	_____	"We**'ve had** a cell phone for 12 years," he said.	He said that they **had had** a cell phone for 12 years.
4.	_____	"I**'ll text** you when I get to the party," he promised.	He promised that he **would text** me when he got to the party.
5.	_____	"I **can send** you an email," she whispered to her friend.	She whispered that she **could send** her friend an email.

> Check your answers: Grammar reference, p. 114

6. Look at the chart in Exercise 5. What does the verb in quoted speech change to in reported speech? Complete the table.

	Quoted speech	Reported speech
1.	Simple present	Simple past
2.	can	_____
3.	Present perfect	_____
4.	Simple past	_____
5.	will	_____

NOTICE IT
In quoted speech, put the comma inside the quotation marks when the quote is first, and outside the quotation marks when the quote comes second.

*"I'm using my computer right **now**," she said.*
*She **said**, "I'm using my computer right now."*

7. Write these sentences in reported speech form.

1. "Social networking sites are a great way to talk to my friends," said Daniel.
   Daniel said that social networking sites were a great way to talk to his friends.

2. "I learned how to create video games," explained Sophie.
   _____

3. Mike announced, "Students can use their cell phones."
   _____

4. "I'll volunteer next Saturday," promised Sarah.
   _____

5. Travis said, "I've never been to Europe."
   _____

Speaking: Face-to-face

8. YOUR TURN Work with a partner. Ask and answer the questions. Make notes of the answers your partner gives.

How often do you see your friends? What do you do together? Will you hang out this weekend?

9. Use your notes from Exercise 8 to write your partner's answers to the questions in reported speech. Then tell another pair of students about your partner.

> Jack said that he saw his friends on weekends and that they usually went to the mall. He said that they would go to the movies this weekend.

BE CURIOUS Find out about social networks. What are the three social networking sites that the video talks about? (Workbook, p. 88)

Discovery EDUCATION
9.1 SOCIAL NETWORKS

> Workbook, pp. 58–59

Unit 9 | 87

Stop chatting and pay ATTENTION!

Listening: Short conversations

1. Work with a partner. Look at the four pictures. Ask and answer the questions.
   1. Where are the people?
   2. What is the relationship between the people in each picture?
   3. What do you think they're talking about?

2. Listen to four short conversations. Match the pictures in Exercise 1 to the conversations.

   1. ____ 2. ____ 3. ____ 4. ____

3. Listen again. Answer the questions.
   1. Nicole doesn't want to study. What does she want to do? Why does her mother think it's important to study hard?
   2. What is Joe texting Steve about? What does Joe think about his soccer skills?
   3. Why did Rachel have to go home? What did Rachel tell Mr. Peterson about the rules?
   4. Where are Paul and Addison going? What did Greg say would happen if they got to the concert early?

Vocabulary: Communication methods

4. Complete the sentences with the correct words. Then listen and check your answers.

blog post	forum	social network post
chatting	✓microblog post	text message
email	phone call	video chat

   1. My brother doesn't like to express himself in really short sentences, so he won't write a *microblog post*. He writes a long _____ every week, though, about whatever he's interested in.
   2. I can hear you pretty well, but I'm having trouble seeing you. I don't think the _____ is working. Let me send you an _____ instead.
   3. There was an article about the dress code on the school's online _____ today. I was _____ with Lisa about it in class, and Mr. Brown asked us to be quiet.
   4. It's been so long since I made a _____. I don't like to talk that much. I'd rather send a _____ from my phone.
   5. I like to write a _____ a few times a day to say how I'm feeling or to share funny videos with my friends.

5. **YOUR TURN** Work with a partner. What forms of communication do you like best? Why?

88 | Unit 9

Grammar: Reported questions

6. Complete the chart.

In reported questions, the verbs usually change tenses as in reported speech.
The word order in reported questions is the same as in an affirmative sentence.

Direct speech questions	Reported questions
"Why **do** you **have** makeup on?"	He asked her why she ___had___ makeup on.
"Which blog post **did** you **read**?"	She asked me which blog post I _____.
"How **have** you **been**?"	He asked me how I _____.
"When **will** you **chat** with me?"	She asked me when I _____ with her.
"Who **can help** them send a text message?"	He asked who _____ them send a text message.
Use if in Yes/No reported questions.	
"Are you on your way?"	He asked **if** we were on our way.
"Did you see what happened?"	She asked _____ I had seen what happened.

> Check your answers: Grammar reference, p. 114

7. Circle the correct answer.

1. "Where is your cell phone?" She asked **if / where** my cell phone was.
2. "Will you write that blog post today?" My teacher asked **if / when** I would write that blog post today.
3. "Can you do a video chat with a cell phone?" My grandmother asked **can / if** I could do a video chat with a cell phone.
4. "What did you do last night during the game?" Leah asked **if / what** I had done last night during the game.

8. Write the sentences as reported questions.

1. Devon asked me, "How are you doing?"

   Devon asked me how I was doing.

2. Nicolas asked John, "Where have you been?"

   _____

3. My parents asked me, "Do you want to eat breakfast?"

   _____

4. I asked my friends, "When can we hang out?"

   _____

Get it RIGHT!

In reported questions, don't use the auxiliary verb *do*.
He asked me how **I created** my website.
NOT: ~~He asked me how did I create my website.~~

Speaking: How often do you turn off your cell phone?

9. Write five questions to ask your friends. Write about these things:

| text | turn off your cell phone | video chat | write blog posts | write microblog posts |

10. YOUR TURN Work with a partner. Ask and answer your questions from Exercise 9.

> Have you ever written a blog post?
>> Yes, I have.

11. Tell another pair of students about the questions your partner asked you.

> Marco asked me if I had ever written a blog post.

Workbook, pp. 60–61

REAL TALK — 9.2 WHAT DO YOU THINK ABOUT CELEBRITY GOSSIP?

That's not what I HEARD!

Conversation: What do you think about celebrity gossip?

1. **REAL TALK** Watch or listen to the teenagers. Write the correct numbers.
   1. _____ of the teenagers said they didn't like celebrity gossip at all.
   2. _____ of the teenagers said that it depended on the situation or the topic.

2. **YOUR TURN** What do you think about celebrity gossip? Where do you hear the gossip you're interested in: social media, TV, online news, or another source?

3. Listen to Zoe and Cole talking about some celebrity news. Complete the conversation.

> **USEFUL LANGUAGE: Comparing different accounts of a story**
> - That's not what I heard!
> - Well, Diana said that
> - That's definitely not what happened.
> - I asked Natalie what had happened, and she said that
> - ✓ According to
> - How did you come up with that idea?

Zoe: ¹ _According to_ Hollywood Tonight, the police arrested Ashley Hill last night.

Cole: I heard that, too.

Zoe: It says that Ashley cut Jonah Clark's hair off while he was asleep, and then stole his car.

Cole: ² _____

Zoe: What? How do you know?

Cole: ³ _____ Ashley had borrowed her boyfriend's car. She didn't steal it. The problem is, she doesn't have a driver's license.

Zoe: She was probably with Shawn Evans when it happened.

Cole: Shawn Evans? ⁴ _____ She doesn't even know Shawn Evans.

Zoe: Yes, she does. They've been friends since they were on that TV show.

Cole: Oh yeah, that's right. Why do you think she was with Shawn last night?

Zoe: ⁵ _____ Shawn and Ashley are more than friends. They started dating about two weeks ago.

Cole: Where did Diana hear that? ⁶ _____ Hollywood Tonight just said that her boyfriend was Jonah Clark!

Zoe: This is pretty confusing. Let's see if Ashley posted anything online about it.

Cole: She can't post anything. She's in jail. Remember?

4. Practice the conversation with a partner.

5. **YOUR TURN** Work with a partner. Take turns comparing different accounts of the story.

> According to this site, Max Marker hit a photographer last night.

Student A	Student B
You read online that your favorite singer got angry and tried to hit a photographer.	You hear from a friend that the photographer got angry and tried to hit your favorite singer.

> No way. That's definitely not what happened. I heard that . . .

90 | Unit 9

ARE CELL PHONES GOOD FOR TEENAGERS?

by Avery Bradley

Twenty years ago, cell phones were mostly used by adults for work. Now, it's almost impossible to find a teenager without one. But are cell phones good for teenagers?

There are many good things about cell phones. First, they help teenagers communicate with friends and family anytime, anywhere. Sending text messages is quick and cheap. Cell phones also help organize your life – you have your calendar, photos, and social networking sites all in one place!

However, there are problems with cell phones, too. For one thing, if you forget to check your phone and miss text messages, your friends might think you're mad at them. In addition, you might not always get a signal, especially if you're not in a city. Finally, using your cell phone all the time can get really expensive.

Overall, I think cell phones are a great way for teenagers to communicate. We just need to be careful when we use them.

Reading to write: An essay about cell phones

6. Look at the title of the essay above. What do you think the essay is about? Read the essay to check.

> ● *Focus on* **CONTENT**
> When you write an essay, you can include this information:
> - An introduction
> - A paragraph with arguments in favor
> - A paragraph with arguments against
> - A conclusion, including your opinion

7. Read Avery's essay again. Answer the questions.
1. How does the writer get the reader's attention in the introduction?
2. How many arguments in favor of cell phones are there?
3. How many arguments against cell phones are there?
4. What is Avery's opinion about cell phones for teenagers?

> ● *Focus on* **LANGUAGE**
> **Introducing a series of arguments**
> *First, In addition, For one thing, also, Finally*

8. Find the phrases from the Focus on Language box in Avery's essay.

9. Complete the sentences with the correct words.

also	finally	First
✓ For one thing	In addition	

1. I recommend this cell phone. ¹ _For one thing_ , it's a smartphone. It's ² _____ on sale, and ³ _____ , it's small and light.
2. The new model has two improvements. ⁴ _____ , it has a lot more memory. ⁵ _____ , the battery will last longer.

Writing: An essay about social networking sites

◯ PLAN
Plan an essay with the title "Are Social Networking Sites a Good Way for Teenagers to Communicate?" Use the list in the Focus on Content box and make notes.

◯ WRITE
Write your essay. Use your answers to Exercises 7 and 8 to help you. Write about 150 words.

◯ CHECK
Can you say "yes" to these questions?
- Have you included all the paragraphs mentioned in the Focus on Content box?
- Have you included words and phrases to introduce a series of arguments?

THE WORLD SPEAKS ONE LANGUAGE

Almost everywhere you go in the world, you see English. It's on signs, advertisements, and on T-shirts. It's everywhere! Online, you see even more English. Why? Because it's a world language: a language known and spoken in lots of countries.

How many people speak and understand English? Statistics show that there are 375 million native speakers of English in the world. In some places, like India, Hong Kong, and Kenya, people speak lots of different languages, and English is one of them. Finally, linguists have said that there are more than a billion people who speak English as a foreign language, and that figure is increasing. In many countries, such as Denmark, Singapore, and Israel, more than 80 percent of the people speak English.

Do you like to travel? International tourists can't speak the language of every country they dream of visiting. Most countries, however, write signs, menus, and tourist pamphlets in at least two languages: the native language of that country and English. Tourists may not speak Arabic, for example, but when they visit Egypt, they can still eat great food, take tours, and have a wonderful time if they speak English.

Online, English is important, too. In 2013, researchers said that 55 percent of the most popular websites used English as their main language. If you set up a blog, for example, more people will find out about you and read your posts if you write in English. Over 95 percent of all scientific articles, either online or published in science magazines, are in English. And that number is growing.

And what about the future? Will English always be the world's number one language? For the moment, yes. But if the Chinese economy continues to grow, will Mandarin turn into the next number one world language? We'll have to wait and see.

DID YOU KNOW...?
Soon there will be more people in China who speak English as a foreign language than there are native English speakers in the whole world.

Culture: The number one language

1. Look at the photo above. Where would you see this sign? Why do you think the sign is in English?
2. Read and listen to the article. Is English still the world's number one language?
3. Read the article again. Are the sentences true (*T*) or false (*F*)?
   1. English is everywhere because it's a world language. ___
   2. About 375 million people speak English as a foreign language. ___
   3. Most countries try to help tourists by creating material in English. ___
   4. Over half of the most popular websites use English as the main language. ___
   5. The author is sure that Mandarin will be the world's next number one language. ___
4. **YOUR TURN** Work with a partner. Ask and answer the questions.
   1. How much English do you see or hear where you live? Where do you see it?
   2. Do you ever use English on the computer or on your phone? What do you use it for?

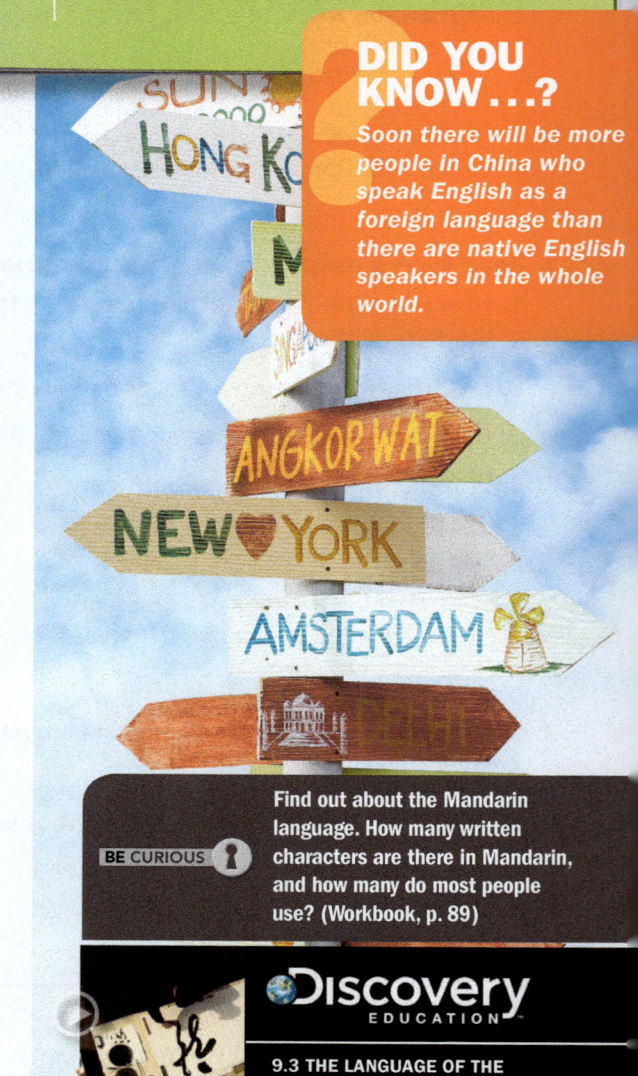

BE CURIOUS Find out about the Mandarin language. How many written characters are there in Mandarin, and how many do most people use? (Workbook, p. 89)

Discovery EDUCATION
9.3 THE LANGUAGE OF THE FUTURE?

UNIT 9 REVIEW

Vocabulary

1. Complete the sentences with the correct words.

| announce | ✓explain | shout |
| complain | remind | whisper |

1. I don't understand our homework. Can you ___explain___ it to me?
2. Ken and Emily often _____ about people who use cell phones all the time. They really don't like it.
3. The fans in the stadium usually _____ so loudly that the other team can't hear instructions from the coach.
4. Please don't talk loudly here! People are studying, and you need to _____.
5. When are the TV stations going to _____ the news about the election?
6. If I don't remember to call my mom, please _____ me.

Grammar

2. Rewrite the sentences below in reported speech.

1. "I'm blogging about the movie."
   She said she was blogging about the movie.
2. "I go online every day."
   He _____.
3. "I can video chat with you tonight."
   She _____.
4. "I have written 100 blog posts."
   He _____.
5. "I am thinking about Daniel."
   She _____.
6. "I will send Paul an email."
   He _____.

3. Rewrite the questions below as reported questions.

1. "Who are you talking to?"
   She _asked who I was talking to._
2. "What is Alicia thinking about?"
   He _____
3. "Do you have Will's phone number?"
   They _____
4. "When will he send them a text message?"
   She _____
5. "Have you posted the picture on your blog?"
   He _____
6. "Who can help her?"
   They _____

Useful language

4. Complete the conversation.

| According to | That's definitely |
| Steve said that | That's not |

Tyler: Hey, Rob. I just heard about Ryan.
Rob: What did you hear?
Tyler: ¹_____ Ryan had been cheating on a test with his cell phone, and Ms. Harris caught him.
Rob: ²_____ not what happened.
Tyler: What do you mean?
Rob: ³_____ Jared, Ryan saw someone else cheating, and he told Ms. Harris about it.
Tyler: Hmm. ⁴_____ what I heard.
Rob: Ryan never cheats. And, I don't think he even has a cell phone. He lost his last week.
Tyler: Well, where is Ryan now? Let's just ask him and find out the truth!

PROGRESS CHECK: Now I can . . .
- ☐ talk about different ways of speaking.
- ☐ discuss social networking.
- ☐ talk about different communication methods.
- ☐ compare stories.
- ☐ write an essay about cell phones.
- ☐ discuss language use throughout the world.

CLIL PROJECT
9.4 PICTURES WITH MEANING, p. 120

10 Don't Give Up!

Discovery EDUCATION

BE CURIOUS

- Lifeguard and Athlete 
- Have you ever given a class presentation? 
- Circus Star

1. Describe what you see in this picture.

2. What do you think this runner did to prepare for the race?

3. Have you ever worked very hard toward a specific goal? What did you do?

UNIT CONTENTS

Vocabulary Goals and achievements; emotions related to accomplishments
Grammar Reflexive pronouns; causative *have/get*
Listening Challenging situations

Vocabulary: Goals and achievements

1. Write the words next to the definitions.

achieve	commitment	face	performance	reward
challenge	✓ deal with	goal	progress	skill

1. To take action to solve a problem: _DEAL WITH_
2. Something you want to do successfully in the future: _ _ _ _
3. How well someone does something: _ _ _ _ _ _ _ _ _ _ _
4. To succeed in doing something good: _ _ _ _ _ _ _
5. To give something in exchange for good behavior or good work: _ _ _ _ _ _
6. To deal with a difficult situation: _ _ _ _
7. An ability to do an activity well because you have practiced it: _ _ _ _ _
8. Development and improvement of skills or knowledge: _ _ _ _ _ _ _ _
9. Something that is difficult and tests your ability: _ _ _ _ _ _ _ _ _
10. A willingness to give your time and energy: _ _ _ _ _ _ _ _ _ _

2. Listen, check, and repeat.

3. Circle the correct answers.

1. You ran 5 kilometers last week and 10 kilometers this week. That's real **progress / goal**!
2. My father **dealt with / achieved** something no one in his family had done before: He went to college and became a doctor.
3. Your **commitment / performance** on this test was incredible. You got 100 percent right!
4. This class isn't easy. It will **challenge / achieve** you to work harder than you've ever worked before.
5. Bianca didn't study for her chemistry test, so she had to **reward / face** the consequences: a bad grade.
6. My **goal / skill** in life isn't to be rich or famous. I just want to be good at what I do.

> **Spell it RIGHT!**
> Notice that *ie* and *ei* can both represent the sound /iː/.
> ach**ie**ve, bel**ie**ve
> c**ei**ling, rec**ei**ve

Speaking: Go for it!

4. YOUR TURN Work with a partner. Ask and answer the questions.

1. What is one academic or personal goal that you have for the next 12 months?
2. Do you have an unusual skill? What is it?
3. Have you ever been challenged to do a difficult or incredible thing? What?

> *One of my academic goals for the next 12 months is to get better grades in science.*

▶ Workbook, p. 64

Reading Make Your Dreams Come True; Achieving My Goal; Olympics for the Brain
Conversation Reassuring someone
Writing A personal action plan

Dream BIG!

Make Your DREAMS Come True

by Kyle Stewart, school counselor at West High School in Franklin, Pennsylvania

In my 22 years as a high school counselor, I've talked to thousands of teenagers. Many of them have goals, from traveling around the world to changing the world. While some teenagers achieve the goals they set for themselves, others don't. If you have a dream, here's how to make it happen:

First, decide on a clear goal. What exactly do you want to do? Make sure it's your dream and not someone else's. Your father wants you to be a doctor. Do you want to be a doctor, too? If you do, great. You will need your own commitment to do the hard work of reaching your long-term goals.

Then choose a date to reach your goal. For example, do you want to go to college a year early? Then you may want to take extra classes now. Set a deadline, and challenge yourself to meet that deadline.

I've found that most people benefit from writing about their goals. A written list reminds people to work on their goals and helps them see their progress! Start by writing down your goal, your deadline, and the steps you need to take to make your dream a reality.

Finally, put your plan into action. Start taking the steps you wrote on your list. You have to do this work yourself. No one can do it for you. Remember to review your written goals at least once a week. And then, dream your dreams and never give up!

Reading: An online article

1. **Look at the title of the article. Do you have a dream that you'd like to come true? What could you do about it?**

2. **Read and listen to the article. Number the steps below in the correct order (1–4).**
   a. ___ Set a date to accomplish your goal.
   b. ___ Make your plan happen.
   c. ___ Decide for yourself what your goal is.
   d. ___ Get a pen and paper and start writing.

3. **Read the article again. Are the sentences true (T) or false (F)?**
   1. Kyle Stewart is a teenager with a dream. ___
   2. All of the students that Kyle talks to achieve their dreams. ___
   3. It's important to make sure that your goal is something you want for yourself. ___
   4. Students should decide a date by which they want to achieve their goal. ___
   5. Writing down the goal is not an important step. ___
   6. Nobody else can put your plan into action. You have to do it. ___

4. **YOUR TURN** Choose one of the goals below or a goal of your own. How could you achieve this goal? Discuss your steps with a partner.

be a scientist	improve your grades	make new friends
get fit and healthy	learn a musical instrument	save the environment

   I want to make some new friends, and I want to do it by the end of this year.

   Maybe you could join a new club!

DID YOU KNOW...?

The first jobs of many famous people were very different from their dreams. Singer Mick Jagger worked in a mental hospital, actress Jennifer Aniston was a telephone salesperson, and actor Tom Hanks sold popcorn and peanuts.

Grammar: Reflexive pronouns

5. Complete the chart.

> *Use a reflexive pronoun when an object refers to the subject.*
>
> **I** like to challenge **myself** by measuring my progress every week.
>
> **You** need to set a deadline for _____.
>
> **He** wasn't pleased with **himself** when he heard criticism of his performance.
>
> **She** taught _____ the skills she needed to write essays.
>
> **We** decided to enjoy **ourselves** only after we had studied for the test.
>
> **Teenagers** can help _____ to any of the career planning books we have.
>
> Many people achieve the goals **they** set for **themselves**.

> Check your answers: Grammar reference, p. 115

6. Complete the sentences.

1. My sister rewarded __herself__ with a long walk after she had studied for three hours.
2. We set _____ a deadline for finishing the big project.
3. I didn't do well on the test. I blame _____ for not studying harder.
4. To succeed in life, you need to believe in _____.
5. Those kids need to face challenges by _____. They can't always ask their parents to help them.
6. Edward scared _____ when he thought he had lost his homework.

7. Add a sentence with a reflexive pronoun and *by*.

1. Nobody in the group had time to work on the presentation except Adrian and Stephanie.
   They worked on it by themselves.
2. He didn't have help writing his essays for school.
   _____
3. Nobody helped Cristina do the project.
   _____
4. None of my friends wanted to study with me yesterday.
   _____
5. My sister and I didn't do our exchange programs together.
   _____
6. My best friend couldn't go shopping yesterday.
   _____

> **Reflexive pronouns with *by***
>
> *You can use reflexive pronouns with by to say you did something "without help" or "alone."*
>
> I don't cook much, but I made this dinner **by myself**. Do you like it?
>
> Mike painted his house **by himself**. He didn't hire a professional painter.

Speaking: Achieve it!

8. YOUR TURN Work with a partner. Choose one of the goals below. Decide on five steps a person needs to take to achieve it.

   a. Win a gold medal in the Olympic Games
   b. Discover a cure for cancer
   c. Win an Oscar for best actor in a movie

> *To win a gold medal, you have to challenge yourself.*

> *Right, but you can't do it all by yourself. You need a coach!*

> **Say it RIGHT!**
>
> 10.03
>
> A consonant cluster is a group of consonants with no vowels. Pay attention to the pronunciation of consonant clusters with /l/. Listen and repeat the words.
> myse**lf**, himse**lf**, themse**lv**es
> ski**lls**, she**lls**, te**lls**

> **BE CURIOUS** Find out about a lifeguard in Australia. What does Candice do to train for the life saving competition? (Workbook, p. 90)
>
> **Discovery EDUCATION**
>
> 10.1 LIFEGUARD AND ATHLETE

Are you up to the CHALLENGE?

Listening: Challenging situations

1. Look at the topics below. How could they be "challenging situations"?
   a. A homemade birthday cake
   b. A video competition
   c. An important test
   d. A soccer championship

2. Listen to four short conversations. Match the topics in Exercise 1 with the conversations.

   1. _____   2. _____   3. _____   4. _____

3. Listen again. Answer the questions.

   1. What did Lauren and her team win? Why isn't Lauren jumping up and down?
   2. What was the name of the competition that David entered? What bad thing happened while David was making the video?
   3. Who is Jennifer making the birthday cake for? What kind of cake is Jennifer's friend going to have made?
   4. Why had Logan missed a lot of school? Where is Logan's dad going to take him?

Vocabulary: Emotions related to accomplishments

4. Complete the sentences with the correct words.

calm	✓ disappointed	miserable	prepared	satisfied
confident	excited	nervous	proud	thrilled

   1. I'm _disappointed_ that I can't be in the play. I really wanted to do it.
   2. After training every day for seven weeks, I know I'm _____ for the race.
   3. I was _____ of my son for doing his homework every day this week.
   4. Sabrina studied really hard for the test, so she was _____ that she would do well.
   5. My sister got an amazing scholarship to a school in Australia. She's _____!
   6. Don't worry so much about your presentation. Just stay _____.
   7. I could get a new bike, but I'm pretty _____ with my old one.
   8. I was so _____ about my new school that I couldn't sleep the night before the first day of classes.
   9. Vince can't go to summer camp this year, and he feels _____ about it.
   10. When I'm _____ about something, I wake up really early and have lots of energy.

5. **YOUR TURN** Choose five words from Exercise 4. For each word, tell a partner about a time you felt that emotion.

Grammar: Causative *have/get*

5. Complete the chart.

Use causative have/get *in situations where someone else does something for you. You don't do it. You can use* get *or* have. *They have similar meanings.*

Lauren is **getting** her knee **examined** now. (She isn't examining her own knee. A doctor is.)

Jennifer **had** a cake _____ for her friend. (She didn't make it. A professional did.)

David needs to **get** his camera _____. (He can't fix it. A professional can.)

Logan will **have** his eyes _____. (He won't check them. A professional will.)

The past participle of get *is* gotten.

Has Sophia **gotten** Jason's cake made yet? No, she hasn't.

> Check your answers: Grammar reference, p. 115

6. Complete the sentences with causative *have/get* and the words in parentheses.

1. Derek gets bad headaches every night when he does his homework. He needs to ___*get his eyes checked*___ (check his eyes).

2. Veronica needed a photo of herself for her passport. She went to a photographer to _____ (take her photo).

3. To look good for the school dance, I'm going to _____ (cut my hair) this afternoon.

4. I'm going to _____ (paint my bedroom) bright pink so that I feel more motivated to study.

5. Your sister is really smart! Has she _____ (test) to see if she has an extra-high IQ?

6. Jim wasn't confident about the game because his shoulder hurt a lot. He should have _____ (examine his shoulder) before the game.

7. Read the situations and write sentences with causative *have/get*.

1. Mitch's only dress shirt is dirty. A dry cleaning company washed it.
   He got his shirt cleaned.

2. My computer is broken, and I really need it. A repair person is going to fix it tomorrow.
   _____

3. The cheerleader hurt her knee. A doctor bandaged it.
   _____

4. The students stayed up late getting their English project ready. A pizza place delivered a pizza to them.
   _____

Speaking: Let's have a party!

8. YOUR TURN Work with a partner. Choose one of the events below. Decide on six steps to make the event happen. You must do three by yourselves, and get other people to do three.

a. You're going to have a birthday party, and you will invite 200 people.

b. You're going to organize a concert where a local band will play for your community.

c. You're in charge of a school trip. Three classes are going together to visit an important monument or nature site outside your city.

> *For this birthday party, we need to get 200 invitations printed.*

> **Get it RIGHT!**
> When you get/have something done, you don't do it yourself.
> I'm going to cut my hair. = I'm going to cut my own hair.
> I'm going to get/have my hair cut. = Another person is going to cut my hair.

> Workbook, pp. 66–67

REAL TALK 10.2 HAVE YOU EVER GIVEN A CLASS PRESENTATION?

You'll do GREAT!

Conversation: Have you ever given a class presentation?

1. **REAL TALK** Watch or listen to the teenagers. Write the numbers 1–6 in the order that you hear about these things.

   a. ___ I'm worried about doing one.
   b. ___ We talked about summer camp.
   c. _1_ I talked about Indonesia last week.
   d. ___ We do one every Friday.
   e. ___ I don't know how to surf.
   f. ___ I talked about my family and friends.

2. **YOUR TURN** Have you ever given a class presentation? What was the best part? What was the worst?

3. Listen to Julia talking to her sister Ella about a presentation. Complete the conversation.

> **USEFUL LANGUAGE: Reassuring someone**
> I think I can help you.
> ✓ You've faced bigger challenges than this!
> Try not to worry about it.
> I'm sure you'll do fine.

Julia: What's the matter, Ella? You look miserable.
Ella: I'm not miserable, just nervous. I have to give a presentation in English class next week, and I'm scared.
Julia: Come on. A presentation?
¹ *You've faced bigger challenges than this!*
Ella: Yeah, but not in English. And never in front of people!
Julia: ² _____ Your English is good.
Ella: Yes, but I'm really shy. And some people in my class speak really great English. I'm worried they'll laugh at me.
Julia: You'll do great.
Ella: No, I won't! When I speak in class, I mix up the words and talk too fast.
Julia: Listen, ³ _____ Have you written the presentation yet?
Ella: Well, most of it. It's almost done.
Julia: Great, then. You can practice it on me and my friends. The more you practice, the better you'll do.
Ella: OK! That sounds like a good idea. I'll feel more confident then.
Julia: Exactly. ⁴ _____ You'll be fine.

4. Practice the conversation with a partner.

5. **YOUR TURN** Work with a partner. Take turns explaining one of the problems and reassuring your partner.
   - You have to sing a song in a talent show.
   - You're playing in the final of a tennis tournament.

Achieving MY GOAL

Posted by Jacob, October 15

In two years, when I'm 17, I am determined to be an exchange student in a Spanish-speaking country. In order to achieve this, I will begin taking Spanish classes next semester at school. I don't speak any Spanish, so I'll have to study hard every day. In addition, I'll do research on different study abroad programs. When I find the best one, and learn about the price and the way it works, I'll talk to my parents. I'll need help from them, and I hope they agree to help! I'll ask them if they can pay for part of the program. I also plan to get a job in the summer – this summer and the next. I'll work as much as I can and keep studying Spanish. Then I'll apply for the exchange program, filling out all the forms and getting all the documents needed. When I'm accepted, I'll apply for my passport, and a visa if necessary. Finally, the program will tell me what country I'm going to – Spain, Mexico, Argentina, or Peru. I'll study about the history and culture of that country. That way, I'll be really prepared.

Reading to write: Jacob's blog post

6. Look at the picture. What do you think Jacob's goal is? Read his action plan and check.

> *Focus on* **CONTENT**
> When you write about a goal, begin by describing your goal clearly. Then describe each step you need to take to achieve your goal. For some of the steps, you may need help from other people. Tell your readers who those people are and how they'll help you.

7. Read Jacob's blog post again. Number the steps (1–7) in the order he will take them.

a. ___ talk to his parents

b. ___ get a job

c. ___ start Spanish classes

d. ___ learn about the country

e. ___ apply for the program

f. ___ research programs

g. ___ apply for a passport and visa

> *Focus on* **LANGUAGE**
> When you write about a personal action plan, you can include some of these phrases:
> *I am determined to . . .*
> *In order to achieve this, I will . . .*
> *In addition, I will . . .*
> *I will need help from . . .*

8. Find the phrases in the Focus on Language box in Jacob's blog post and underline the entire sentence.

Writing: A personal action plan

☐ **PLAN**
Choose a goal you'd like to achieve. Write what the goal is and at least five steps toward achieving the goal.

☐ **WRITE**
Write your personal action plan. Use your notes from above to help you. You can also use Jason's blog post as a model.

☐ **CHECK**
Check your writing. Can you say "yes" to these questions?
- Is your goal described clearly?
- Did you write at least five steps toward your goal?

Olympics for the Brain

Do you want to win medals and earn scholarships? These things are not just for great athletes, but for hard-working students, too. How? Form a team and join Academic Decathlon®!

What is Academic Decathlon®?
It's an academic competition for students from all over the United States, and sometimes all over the world. Every year, teams of students study one topic – past themes have included Russia, the Great Depression, and energy alternatives. Then they compete in local, state, and national championships.

Who is on each team?
Teams include nine students, and each team must have three different types of students on it. Three members must be excellent students. Three members must be students who do well, but who aren't the school's top students. And three team members must be students who don't get great grades.

What happens in the competition?
Competitions aren't about being good at one subject area only. Every team member needs to be prepared to do five things. First, they need to deliver a speech related to the topic, and then answer questions. Then students need to answer questions about themselves in an interview. After that, they need to write an essay about the topic. They also need to take seven different tests in subject areas related to the topic. And finally, teams participate in a Super Quiz. Teams listen to questions and have seven seconds to answer them. It's the only part of the competition open to the public, and it's noisy, fun, and exciting.

Why do students love Academic Decathlon®?
Lots of reasons! Like athletes, these students enjoy working as a team. If you join a team, you'll meet other students from all over the country, and work very hard to get there. Most of all, you'll have fun!

Culture: United States Academic Decathlon®

1. **Answer the questions.**
   1. Have you ever won a medal? What was it for?
   2. Would you be interested in participating in an academic competition?

2. **Read and listen to the article. What kinds of students can participate in Academic Decathlon®?**

3. **Read the article again. Answer the questions.**
   1. Where do the students who compete come from?
   2. How many people are on a team?
   3. Do team members need to learn about one subject area or all subject areas?
   4. What do students have to answer questions about in the interview?
   5. Which part of the competition can the public watch?

4. **YOUR TURN** Work with a partner. Ask and answer the questions.
   1. What kind of academic competitions can you compete in where you live?
   2. Would you enjoy participating in Academic Decathlon®? What part of it sounds most interesting to you?

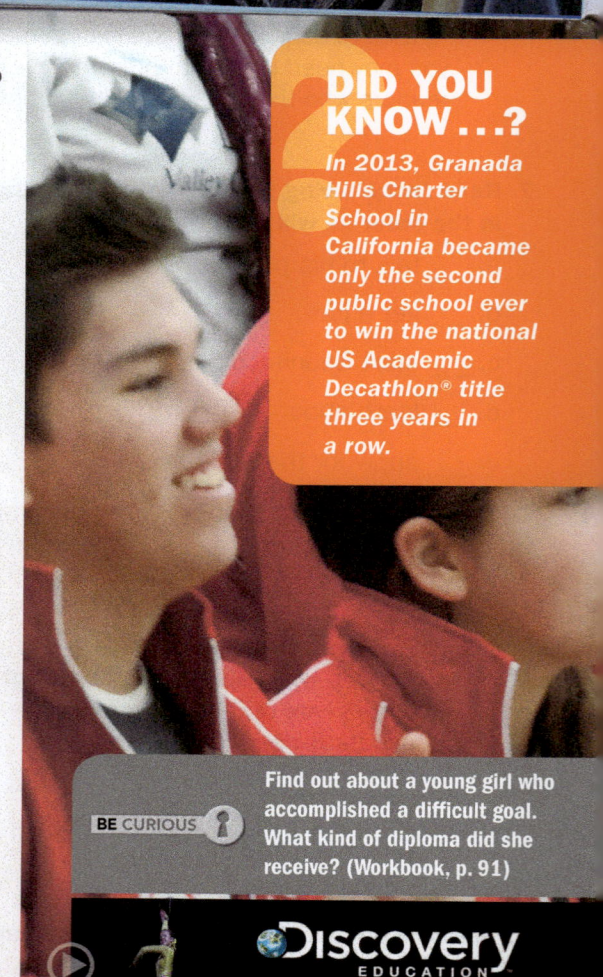

DID YOU KNOW...?
In 2013, Granada Hills Charter School in California became only the second public school ever to win the national US Academic Decathlon® title three years in a row.

BE CURIOUS Find out about a young girl who accomplished a difficult goal. What kind of diploma did she receive? (Workbook, p. 91)

Discovery EDUCATION
10.3 CIRCUS STAR

UNIT 10 REVIEW

Vocabulary

1. Complete the sentences.

challenge	goal	rewarded
face	progress	✓ skills

1. Academic Decathlon® helps students develop their public speaking ___skills___.
2. When you want to accomplish an important _____, it's a good idea to write it down and look at it often.
3. Caleb doesn't like to do only easy things. He likes to _____ himself.
4. After several students in my class won an academic competition, the school _____ the whole class with a party.
5. You won't achieve your goal right away, but you can make a little _____ toward it every day.
6. Instead of ignoring or running away from your problems, it's always better to _____ them directly.

Grammar

2. Complete the sentences with reflexive pronouns.

1. After doing homework for seven hours on Saturday, Greta rewarded ___herself___ by going to a movie with her best friend.
2. What happened to his finger? Did he cut _____?
3. Even though I had a bad headache, I forced _____ to study hard.
4. Sarah and Olivia love math, and they challenge _____ to always learn more.
5. When we were little, my brother and I used to pretend we were astronauts. We called _____ "The Moon Boys."

3. Circle the correct answers.

1. When I decided to start exercising before school each morning, the first thing I did was ____.
   a. get fixed my alarm clock
   b. (have my alarm clock fixed)

2. Charles won a silver medal in the Olympics. When he came home, he ____.
   a. got it framed   b. have framed it

3. Jada accidentally stepped on her cell phone and needed to ____.
   a. repair   b. get it repaired

4. When are you going to ____? You need to do it soon, I think.
   a. take your passport picture
   b. get your passport picture taken

5. When my sister graduated from high school, my parents had a big party for her. They ____.
   a. had a big chocolate cake made
   b. make a big chocolate cake

Useful language

4. Complete the conversation.

| I'm sure | I think I can | worry about it | you've faced |

Matt: Dad, I'm really nervous. I want to try out for the basketball team tomorrow, but I've never played basketball except out in the driveway with you!

Dad: [1]_____ you'll do fine. Science nerds can play sports too, you know.

Matt: I don't know. I'm tall, but I'm not as tall as some of those guys. And they're all really good.

Dad: Basketball isn't all about height. Try not to [2]_____ and just do your best.

Matt: Don't worry? That's all I do. I don't think I can do this.

Dad: Listen, [3]_____ bigger challenges than this. Remember last year's science fair? That was harder than basketball tryouts.

Matt: No, I don't think so. I'm good at science.

Dad: [4]_____ help you. Let's go outside and practice together.

Matt: OK. Thanks!

PROGRESS CHECK: Now I can . . .

☐ talk about goals and accomplishments.
☐ discuss emotions related to accomplishments.
☐ discuss steps toward achieving goals.
☐ reassure someone.
☐ write a personal action plan.
☐ discuss an academic competition.

Uncover Your Knowledge

UNITS 6–10 Review Game

TEAM 1
START

1. Imagine you have a chance to meet a celebrity, living or dead. Use the second conditional to tell your teammate who you would meet and what you would do.

2. Name five things that can happen in school.

3. Think of two imaginary situations and ask your teammate what they would do in those situations.

4. Say eight different materials that things can be made from.

5. Identify four items in your classroom. Say what two of them are made of and what the other two are used for.

6. Imagine that you saw a classmate cheating on a test. Explain the situation to your teammate and ask for advice on what to do about it.

7. Tell your teammate how you would design and build an eco-friendly building. What would it be? How it would save energy?

8. Ask your teammate two questions in the simple past passive. Use Where, When, How, or Who. Your teammate answers with a simple past passive statement.

9. In 30 seconds, say two phrases that use the verb *do* and two phrases that use the verb *make*.

10. What had you known about extreme weather disasters before this unit? Tell your teammate two things you had known, and two things you hadn't known.

11. Tell a teammate that he or she has done something that upset you. Your teammate apologizes.

INSTRUCTIONS:

- Make teams and choose game pieces.
- Put your game pieces on your team's START.
- Flip a coin to see who goes first.
- Read the first challenge. Can you do it correctly?

   Yes → Continue to the next challenge.

   No → Lose your turn.

The first team to do all of the challenges wins!

GRAMMAR

VOCABULARY

USEFUL LANGUAGE

TEAM 2
START

Tell a teammate two things you did, one before the other. Use the past perfect and simple past.

Role-play a conversation with your teammate. Tell them about a personal problem, and have them try to help you.

What three items would you want to have if you were lost in the woods? Explain why.

Report to your teammate three different things you heard people say yesterday.

How do you feel when you are getting ready for a big test? How do you feel when the test is over and you did well? Use at least four emotion words.

In 30 seconds, say three sentences that use reflexive pronouns.

Name at least one natural disaster that can occur in each area: forests, mountains, tropical islands, and flat areas.

Say three phrases you can use to reassure someone.

Have your teammate ask you a question. Then tell another teammate what your first teammate asked you.

Give six examples of verbs you can use to report speech in 30 seconds.

Role-play a conversation with your teammate. Say that something happened to a celebrity last night. Your teammate heard a different version of the story. Compare your stories.

Describe a goal you have achieved. Tell your teammate what your goal was, what challenges you faced, and how you dealt with them.

Use causative have/get to tell your teammate three things that other people do for you.

List all the different ways you communicated with people this week.

Units 6–10 Review | 105

Simple present and present continuous review, page 5

Use the simple present to describe what normally happens. This includes routines and facts.

It **sticks** to your face.	He/She/It **doesn't** live here.
I/You/We/They **like** cold weather.	I/You/We/They **don't like** hot weather.
I/You/We/They **get** home late.	I/You/We/They **don't go out** a lot.

Use the present continuous to describe something happening right now or these days.

I'm **wearing** a hat.	I'm **not wearing** boots.
He/She **is working** right now.	He/She **isn't studying** right now.
You/We/They **are eating** hot food these days.	You/We/They **aren't drinking** coffee.

1. Write sentences in the simple present or the present continuous.

1. it / always / rain / in April _____
2. Tonya / write / a paper right now _____
3. they / not walk / to work these days _____
4. I / eat / dinner at 6:00 p.m. every night _____
5. Jack / not like / subzero weather _____
6. we / play / soccer outside right now _____

Simple past and past continuous review, page 7

Use the simple past to describe actions and events in the past.

I/You/He/She/We/They **took** a plane over part of Panama.
I/You/He/She/We/They **didn't have** to stop for food.
I/You/He/She/We/They **started** the trip in Alaska.
I/You/He/She/We/They **didn't start** the trip in California.
We **made** our own food.
He **didn't break** his arm, but it hurt a lot.
What **did** you **miss** the most?

Use the past continuous to describe actions and events in progress in the past.

I **was spending** the night in Quito when I <u>heard</u> that the road was closed.
He **wasn't wearing** a helmet when he <u>fell</u>.
We **were riding** through Colorado when Robert <u>hurt</u> his arm.
They **were eating** their lunch by the road when the storm <u>started</u>.
You **weren't talking** to me when I <u>dropped</u> my phone.
What **were** you **doing** last night when the electricity <u>went</u> out?

2. Complete the sentences with the simple past or past continuous.

1. Jackie _____ (ride) her bike when she _____ (fall).
2. We _____ (give) a lot of money to an education program last year.
3. Paul and Oliver _____ (watch) TV when it _____ (start) to hail.
4. I _____ (not study) when you _____ (call) me.
5. My sisters _____ (not do) their homework when I _____ (get) home.
6. She _____ (hear) about the blizzard at 10:00 a.m.

have to/don't have to, page 15

Use have/has to to say that it is necessary to do something. Use don't/doesn't have to to say that it is not necessary to do something, but you can do it if you want to.	
Affirmative	**Negative**
I/You/We/They **have to get** more sleep.	I/You/We/They **don't have to get up** early on Saturdays.
He/She **has to get up** early on Saturdays.	He/She **doesn't have to help** with the housework.

1. Write sentences with the correct form of *have to*. ✔ = yes, ✗ = no.
   1. I / have / more time for myself / ✔ _____
   2. Ben / help / around the house / ✔ _____
   3. Carol / shop / for clothes this weekend / ✗ _____
   4. They / get up / early tomorrow / ✔ _____
   5. You / work / late tonight / ✗ _____
   6. She / wash / the dishes / ✗ _____

Modals of obligation – *should, ought to, had better,* page 17

Should, ought to, and *had better* have similar meanings. Use them to say what is a good or right thing to do.
Use *should* and *shouldn't* for a personal opinion.
I/You/He/She/We/They **should try** to work out more.
I/You/He/She/We/They **shouldn't get** so stressed out.
Use *ought to* and *ought not to* when you're talking about duty or the law.
I/You/He/She/We/They **ought to call** the police about the car accident.
I/You/He/She/We/They **ought not to enter** that part of the airport.
Use *had better* and *had better not* to give very strong advice.
I/You/He/She/We/They **had better start** studying now.
I/You/He/She/We/They **had better not be** late for the test tomorrow.

2. Complete the sentences with the affirmative or negative of the word or phrase in parentheses.
   1. Kyle _____ relax. He's too stressed out about school. (should)
   2. You _____ apologize to Jenny. You made her feel terrible. (had better)
   3. Vic and Mary _____ go camping. They have a lot of homework this weekend. (should)
   4. We _____ tell your parents about what happened. They need to know. (ought to)
   5. They _____ take their cameras to the museum. You can't take photos there. (ought to)
   6. Jen _____ call Frank right now. He's at a job interview. (had better)

Verb + -ing form (gerund) review, page 25

We can use the -ing form of a verb after some verbs to talk about things we like or don't like.

Common verbs followed by -ing forms:
like, love, hate, enjoy, (not) mind

	-ing form		
I/You/We/They	love	drawing	pictures in my free time.
	don't like	going	to museums.
He/She	enjoys	looking	at sculptures.
	hates	helping	around the house.
	doesn't mind	doing	housework.

1. Complete the conversations with the correct form of the verbs in the box.

   | don't like / go   enjoy / meet   hate / do   love / work   not mind / look |

   1. **A:** Does your brother like art?
      B: Not really, but he _____ at murals.
   2. **A:** Who washes the dishes at your house?
      B: I do. And I _____ it!
   3. **A:** How is your brother's new job?
      B: Great. He _____ at the pizza place.
   4. **A:** Did you see the new sculpture at the museum?
      B: No, I didn't. I _____ to museums.
   5. **A:** Isn't your mother an artist? Could you introduce me to her?
      B: Sure. She _____ new people.

-ing forms (gerunds) as subjects, page 27

You can use the -ing form as the subject of a sentence. The verb is singular.

Playing several instruments at once <u>takes</u> a lot of energy.
Singing at the same time I play instruments <u>is</u> hard.
Being here at the festival <u>is</u> really special to me.

For the negative, use not before the -ing form.

Not enjoying some kinds of music <u>is</u> normal.
Not playing music <u>makes</u> me sad.

2. Put the words in the correct order to make sentences.

   1. is / the trumpet / playing / difficult
      _____

   2. me into trouble / practicing / the piano / gets / not
      _____

   3. easy / finding / isn't / a good keyboard player
      _____

   4. before a concert / it hard to play the flute / makes / eating
      _____

   5. getting / ruins / a good night's sleep / not / my day
      _____

108 | Unit 3

Present perfect with *already*, *yet*, and *just*, page 35

We can use **already** *in affirmative sentences in the present perfect.*
I/You/We/They **have already been** at sea for four days.
He/She **has already cooked** three meals for the others on the ship.
The ship/It **has already left** the port.
We can use **yet** *in negative sentences in the present perfect.*
I/You/We/They **haven't found** turtles **yet**.
He/She **hasn't visited** the ship **yet**.
It **hasn't rained yet**.
Use **just** *with the present perfect to say that something happened very recently.*
I/You/We/They **have just seen** dolphins.
He/She **has just boarded** the ship.
It **has just gotten** dark.

1. **Circle the correct words to complete the sentences.**
   1. Donna has **just** / **yet** bought a mountain bike.
   2. I've **already** / **yet** gone sailing twice this summer.
   3. Carlos and Doug haven't left for summer camp **just** / **yet**.
   4. She hasn't gone on a safari **already** / **yet**.
   5. We've **already** / **just** packed our suitcases for the cruise. We packed them a week ago!
   6. It has **just** / **yet** started raining, so we can't go ballooning now.

Present perfect with *for* and *since*, page 37

Use the present perfect with **for** *or* **since** *for past actions and events continuing into the present.*
Use **for** *with a period of time such as a week, two months, or five years.*
I/You/We/They **have been** here **for** three days.
I/You/We/They **haven't seen** Tom **for** three days.
He/She **has worked** at the rafting company **for** a month.
He/She **hasn't gone** on a trip **for** two years.
Use **since** *with a specific date or time.*
I/You/We/They **have been** here **since** last Wednesday.
I/You/We/They **haven't taken** a vacation **since** last June.
He/She **has lived** in Colorado **since** 2010.
He/She **hasn't called** me **since** last Monday.

2. **Complete the sentences with the present perfect of the verbs in parentheses and *for* or *since*.**
   1. Mario _____ (known) Josh _____ two years.
   2. Ken and Lisa _____ (not eat) _____ 8:00 a.m.
   3. We _____ (wait) for Cindy _____ an hour.
   4. I _____ (live) in Mexico _____ 2008.
   5. You _____ (not see) me _____ three weeks.

Future review – *will*, *be going to*, present continuous, page 45

Use will, be going to, *and the present continuous to talk about the future.*

Use will *for actions and events that we decide to do in the moment of speaking.*

Are you going running now? I **will go** with you.

I/You/He/She/We/They **will go** to the park.

I/You/He/She/We/They **won't go** to the store.

Use going to *for planned actions and events. They may be in the near future or in a more distant future time.*

I'm **(not) going to share** a room with other students.

He/She **is (not) going to fly** to Las Vegas next month.

You/We/They **are (not) going to be** in different schools next year.

Use the present continuous for planned actions and events, usually in the very near future.

I **am (not) traveling** to New York soon.

He/She **is (not) having** dinner with her mother tonight.

You/We/They **are (not) going** to the wedding tomorrow.

Be going to *is used much more than* will *in conversation.*

1. Complete the sentences with the given form of the verbs in parentheses.

1. Kendra _____ a test tomorrow. (take – *present continuous*)
2. Wait for me! I _____ ready in five minutes. (be – *will*)
3. Sally and Mark _____ a movie tonight. (not see – *going to*)
4. He _____ to Rio de Janeiro tonight. (not fly – *present continuous*)
5. My cousins _____ me at the circus on Friday. (meet – *going to*)

Modals of probability – *must, can't, may, might, could*, page 47

Use must *for something you're almost certain of.*
Use can't *for something you believe is impossible.*
Use might, may, *and* could *for something that you believe is possible.*

I/You/He/She/It/We/They	**must be** really terrifying.
	must be terrified.
	must not be relaxed.
	can't be from France.
	may/might/could be upstairs.
	may/might not go to the barbecue.
	may/might/could be sick.

2. Circle the correct answer. Sometimes more than one answer is possible.

1. I ____ be in class tomorrow. I don't feel well.
   a. could   b. might not   c. must   d. may not

2. You ____ be exhausted. You only slept an hour last night.
   a. can't   b. must not   c. must   d. might not

3. Eva ____ be confused about our homework. She just explained it to me.
   a. can't   b. could   c. may   d. might not

4. We ____ go on the roller coaster. I don't think we're tall enough.
   a. must   b. might not   c. may not   d. could

5. They ____ be surprised. They knew we were planning a party.
   a. could   b. may   c. can't   d. might

Second conditional, page 57

Use the second conditional to describe imaginary situations and possible consequences.

Imaginary situation	Possible consequences
if + simple past	*would (not)* + base form of the verb
If I **changed** the school rules,	students **wouldn't wear** uniforms.
If you **missed** class,	you **would be** assigned to detention.
If she **didn't** like the class,	she **wouldn't go**.

Many American English speakers use *were* rather than *was* after *I, he, she,* and *it,* especially in a more formal style.

Formal style	Informal style
If I **were** rude to my teacher, my parents would be very mad at me.	If I **was** always punctual, I wouldn't be assigned to detention so much.

The *if* clause can come at the beginning or end of the sentence. If it's at the beginning, it's followed by a comma.

If you missed class**,** she would be assigned to detention.

You would be assigned to detention **if** you missed class.

1. Write second conditional sentences.

   1. If / you / break / the rules / you / be sent / to the principal's office

   _____

   2. If / Sara / not wear / her uniform / she / be assigned / to detention

   _____

   3. Carl / not get / extra credit / if / he / cheat / on the assignment

   _____

   4. We / be / in trouble / if / we / bully / students

   _____

Second conditional *Wh-* questions, page 59

Use *Wh-* questions in the second conditional to ask about imaginary situations and possible consequences.

What	would your teacher do	if	one of your classmates **cheated** on a test?
Who	would you talk to	if	you **had** a serious problem with a friend?
When	would you go to school	if	you **chose** the days you went?
If	you wanted to do something fun this weekend,	where	would you **go**?
If	you got a new pet,	why	would you **choose** one kind of pet over another?

2. Complete the second conditional questions with *what, who, when,* or *where* and the words in parentheses. Use each question word once.

   1. _____ (you / do) if _____ (you / have) a difficult test to study for?

   2. If _____ (Sheri / go) to New York, _____ (she / go)? In the summer?

   3. If _____ (you / have) a party, _____ (it / be)? At a restaurant or at your house?

   4. _____ (you / ask) for help if _____ (you / not understand) your homework? Your teacher or your friend?

Unit 6 | 111

Simple present passive, page 67

Use the passive when it is not important who does the action, or when you don't know who does it.

To form the simple present passive, use is/are + past participle.

Active	Passive
Affirmative	
They **make** this wall of bottles.	This wall **is made** of bottles.
People **use** car tires to build strong walls.	Car tires **are used** to build strong walls.
Negative	
They **don't make** that bottle of plastic.	That bottle **isn't made** of plastic.
People **don't build** the houses with bricks.	The houses **aren't built** with bricks.

1. Complete the sentences in the simple present passive with the verbs from the box.

   | call | make | not build | not grow | recycle |

   1. The blocks _____ of cement.
   2. This cotton _____ in cold places.
   3. Those plastic bottles _____ to make furniture.
   4. These houses _____ quickly. It takes a long time.
   5. The new exhibit at the museum _____ "Reused Art."

Simple past passive, page 69

Use the passive when it is not important who did the action, or when you don't know who did it.

To form the simple past passive, use was/were + past participle.

Active	Passive
Affirmative	
We **built** the EcoHouse in 1985.	The EcoHouse **was built** in 1985.
We **updated** the appliances two months ago.	The appliances **were updated** two months ago.
Negative	
We **didn't install** a recycling bin until last year.	A recycling bin **wasn't installed** until last year.
They **didn't install** solar panels 60 years ago.	Solar panels **weren't installed** 60 years ago.
Use by with the passive to show who did the action.	
The EcoHouse **was designed by** the museum.	
The most energy **was consumed by** the heater.	
Questions and answers with the passive	
When **was** the EcoHouse **built**?	It **was built** in 1985.
Was the EcoHouse **built** in 1985?	Yes, it **was**.
Were the old apartments **destroyed** this year?	No, they **weren't**.

2. Complete the conversations with the simple past passive.

   1. **A:** _____ the program _____ (install) on your computer?
      B: Yes, it _____. It _____ (do) yesterday by the computer tech.
   2. **A:** Where _____ the pottery _____ (discover)?
      B: It _____ (find) in a pyramid. Then it _____ (take) to a lab by an archeologist. It _____ (not put) in a museum.
   3. **A:** _____ the houses _____ (build) in the 1990s?
      B: No, they _____. They _____ (made) in the 1980s.

Past perfect, page 77

Use the past perfect to refer to something that happened before a specific time in the past.
To form the past perfect, use **had** + past participle.

Affirmative	Negative
I/You/He/She/We/They **had read** a book about it.	I/You/He/She/We/They **hadn't heard** about it before then.
I/You/He/She/It/We/They **had been** fairly quiet for several years.	I/You/He/She/It/We/They **hadn't been** there before.
What **had** I/you/he/she/we/they **heard** about volcanoes before?	
Why **hadn't** I/you/he/she/we/they **researched** anything about Indonesia before?	

Contractions   had = **'d**   had not = **hadn't**

1. Write sentences and questions in the past perfect.

1. Carolina / hear / about the tornado before her parents / .
   _____
2. what / you / learn / tsunamis before class / ?
   _____
3. Tyler / not read / about the forest fires before / .
   _____
4. they / flown / out of the city before the earthquake / .
   _____
5. why / you / not bring / your bike inside before the hurricane / ?
   _____

Past perfect and simple past, page 79

The young man's parents **called** the police after he **had been** gone for three days.
The boy **had drunk** the liquid from all the contact lens cases when they **found** him.
The boy **didn't tell** his story until he **had drunk** a lot of water.

1. We **can** use the past perfect and the simple past in the same sentence.
2. We use the **past perfect** for the action that was completed first.

2. Write sentences with the information in the chart. Use the past perfect and the simple past and the words in parentheses.

First Activity	Second Activity
1. they put on sunscreen	they go to the beach
2. I not buy a sleeping bag	my friend ask me to go camping
3. she cut her arm	she find the first-aid kit
4. we get lost	we not look at the map
5. he not find his flashlight	the lights went out

1. (before) _____
2. (when) _____
3. (after) _____
4. (until) _____
5. (before) _____

Quoted speech vs. reported speech, page 87

Use reported speech to tell others what another person said.

	Quoted speech	Reported speech
Simple present	"It **isn't** right," she said.	She said that it **wasn't** right.
Simple past	"We **spent** the whole day together," she told me.	She told me that they **had spent** the whole day together.
Present perfect	"We**'ve had** a cell phone for 12 years," he said.	They said that they **had had** a cell phone for 12 years.
Future with *will*	"I**'ll text** you when I get to the party," he promised.	He promised that he **would text** me when he got to the party.
can	"I **can send** you an email," she whispered.	She whispered that she **could send** him an email.
Present continuous	"I**'m texting** my friends," he explained.	He explained that he **was texting** his friends.
Past continuous	"I **was checking** my email," she said.	She said that she **had been checking** her email.

1. Read the quoted speech. Then circle the correct answer in the reported speech.

1. "I'll clean my room tomorrow." Leo said that he **could clean** / **would clean** his room tomorrow.
2. "I didn't do my homework." Todd explained that he **hadn't done** / **wouldn't do** his homework.
3. "I'm terrified of earthquakes." Julie announced that she **was** / **will be** terrified of earthquakes.
4. "I can help you." My sister promised me that she **helped** / **could help** me.

Reported questions, page 89

In reported questions, the verbs usually change tenses as in reported speech. The word order in reported questions is the same as in an affirmative sentence.

Direct speech questions	Reported questions
"Why **do** you **have** makeup on?"	He asked her why she **had** makeup on.
"Which blog post **did** you **read**?"	She asked me which blog post I **had read**.
"How **have** you **been**?"	He asked me how I **had been**.
"When **will** you **chat** with me?"	She asked me when I **would chat** with her.
"Who **can help** them send a text message?"	He asked who **could help** them send a text message.
"What **are** you **doing**?"	He asked me what I **was doing**.
"Where **were** you **going**?"	She asked me where I **had been going**.

Use **if** *in Yes/No reported questions.*

"Are you on your way?"	He asked **if** we were on our way.
"Did you see what happened?"	She asked **if** I had seen what happened.

2. Put the words in the correct order to make reported questions.

1. why / she sent her / Yolanda / so many text messages / asked Maria

   _____

2. asked / I / if / my friend / on my blog post / he would comment

   _____

3. forum / asked Sue / which / she had joined / Lorenzo

   _____

114 | Unit 9

Reflexive pronouns, page 97

Use a reflexive pronoun when an object refers to the subject.

I like to challenge **myself** by measuring my progress every week.
You need to set a deadline for **yourself**.
All of **you** should challenge **yourselves** at this job.
He wasn't pleased with **himself** when he heard criticism of his performance.
She taught **herself** the skills she needed to write essays.
We decided to enjoy **ourselves** only after we had studied for the test.
Teenagers can help **themselves** to any of the career planning books we have.
Many people achieve the goals **they** set for **themselves**.
An education is important, and **it** can pay for **itself** if you get a good job.

1. Circle the correct answers.
   1. Maria taught **herself** / **myself** / **himself** to play the piano.
   2. You should reward **ourselves** / **yourself** / **myself** for your hard work.
   3. My parents usually deal with their problems **yourself** / **themselves** / **ourselves**.
   4. Please don't help me. I want to do it by **myself** / **herself** / **yourself**.
   5. Liz and I are very pleased with **herself** / **themselves** / **ourselves**.
   6. Will Eddie teach **myself** / **himself** / **yourself** the computer skills he needs?

Causative *have/get*, page 99

Use causative have/get *in situations where someone else does something for you. You don't do it.*
You can use get *or* have. *They have similar meanings.*

	have/get	object	past participle	
Lauren	is **getting**	her knee	**examined**	now.
Jennifer	**had**	a cake	**made**	for her friend.
David	needs to **get**	his camera	**fixed**.	
Logan	will **have**	his eyes	**checked**.	

2. Write sentences about what Sandy did yesterday and what she will do tomorrow.

Yesterday	Tomorrow
have / tablet / fix	have / hair / cut
get / clothes / clean	get / elbow / examine
get / homework / check	have / bike / repair

1. *Sandy* _____
2. *She* _____
3. _____
4. _____
5. _____
6. _____

CLIL PROJECT

The San PEOPLE

1. Label the pictures with the correct words.

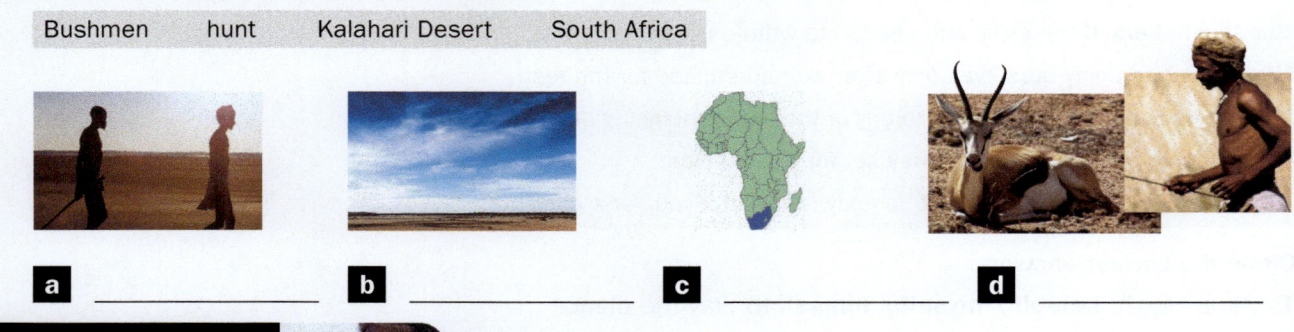

Bushmen   hunt   Kalahari Desert   South Africa

a _____   b _____   c _____   d _____

Discovery EDUCATION
1.4 LIFE IN THE DESERT

2. Watch the video. Complete the phrases with the correct adjectives.

animal   bright   difficult   high   young

1. _____ temperatures
2. a _____ place to live
3. a _____ future
4. _____ tracks
5. a _____ springbok

3. Match the phrases to make sentences.

1. The Kalahari Desert _____
2. The San people have lived _____
3. Recently the South African government _____
4. They get their food _____
5. From the footprints, _____

a. from plants and animals.
b. Isaac can tell the size of the animal.
c. in the Kalahari for thousands of years.
d. is a place of high temperatures and little rain.
e. gave a part of the Kalahari to the Khomani San.

▼ **PROJECT** Learn about a group of people who live close to nature. Some choices are: the Inuit, the Saami, Australian Aborigines, or native South Americans in the Amazon rain forest. Find out more about them and answer the questions below. Present your information to the class.

- What is their name?
- Where do they live?
- What kinds of food are popular in the region?
- How do they get food?
- What kinds of animals live in the region?
- What are some difficulties of living in the region?
- What festivals or celebrations do they have?
- How is their life changing?

Renaissance GREATS

1. Label the pictures with the correct words.

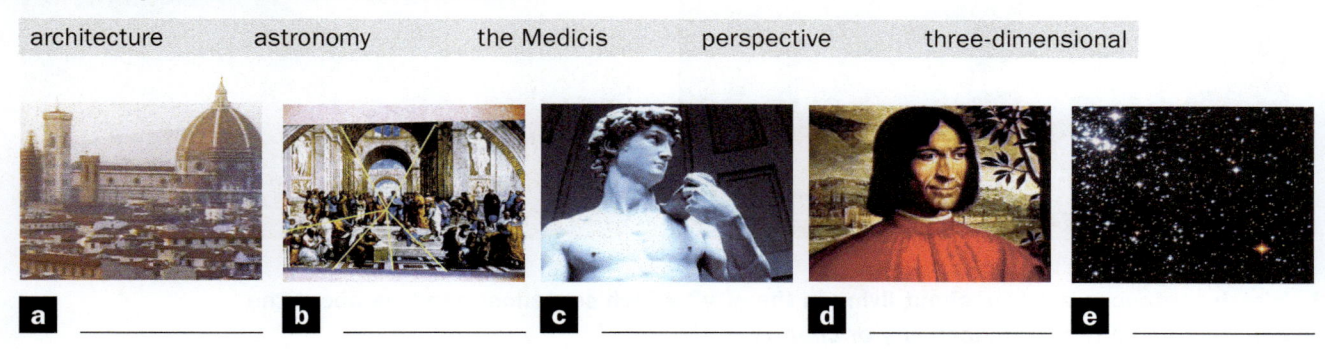

| architecture | astronomy | the Medicis | perspective | three-dimensional |

a _____ b _____ c _____ d _____ e _____

2. Watch the video. Put the sentences 1–6 in the correct categories.

Medieval   Renaissance

_____   _____
_____   _____
_____   _____

1. Paintings didn't look realistic.
2. Rich families gave a lot of money to artists.
3. Paintings looked flat.
4. More important things were bigger in paintings.
5. Paintings were as realistic as possible.
6. Paintings looked three-dimensional.

3. Complete the paragraph with the correct words.

| created | painters | painting | perspective | realistic |

Across Europe, [1]_____ began to use [2]_____ in their work. Filippo Brunelleschi was the first Italian to do this. He [3]_____ a [4]_____ of this building that looked exactly like the real thing. This was the beginning of [5]_____ art.

PROJECT

Leonardo da Vinci, Michelangelo, Filippo Brunelleschi – these are three great artists of the Renaissance. Choose one of them, or think of another, and make a poster. Include the following information on your poster, and then present to your class.

- A picture of your artist
- The years they lived
- Two interesting facts about their life
- A picture of a painting or a building they created
- Describe two things they painted, built, created, or discovered

CLIL PROJECT

Guided TOURS

1. Which sentences are true about living in the city? Which sentences are true about the country? Label the sentences *city* or *country*.

1. There are more things to do, during the day and at night. _____
2. You can enjoy the beauties of nature. _____
3. The streets can be crowded and noisy. _____
4. Sometimes people try to steal your money. _____
5. You know your neighbors and other people. _____
6. People are friendlier and say hello to you. _____
7. Places like schools and hospitals are closer to your home. _____

Discovery EDUCATION
5.4 CITY OR COUNTRY?

2. Watch the video. Complete the sentences with the correct words.

| big | cultural | fashionable | freezing | quiet | small | stylish |

1. In Russia, many people live in the countryside or in _____ towns.
2. But recently, more and more people are moving from the countryside to _____ cities.
3. There are _____ shops and _____ restaurants.
4. But there are some _____ places in cities.
5. In Moscow, people can relax by the river – even in the _____ months of winter.
6. _____ events bring people together.

PROJECT

Write a guide to your city or town. Tell visitors what's different about your part of the world. Use the questions below.

Why go? Give three reasons.
_____

How do you get there? Describe the best routes by plane, train, bus, and car.
_____

What can you see? Name three things.
_____

What can you do? Describe two activities.
_____

Rethinking the CAR

1. Match the words with the correct definitions.

1. _____ fossil fuel
2. _____ carbon dioxide
3. _____ the environment
4. _____ battery
5. _____ renewable energy
6. _____ solar power

a. electricity that comes from the sun's heat
b. energy that comes from the sun, water, or wind
c. fuel from under the ground, like gas, coal, and oil
d. it gives energy to make radios, cars, and toys work
e. the air, water, or land where people, animals, and plants live
f. we produce this gas when we burn things or when we breathe out

2. Watch the video. Complete the sentences with the correct words.

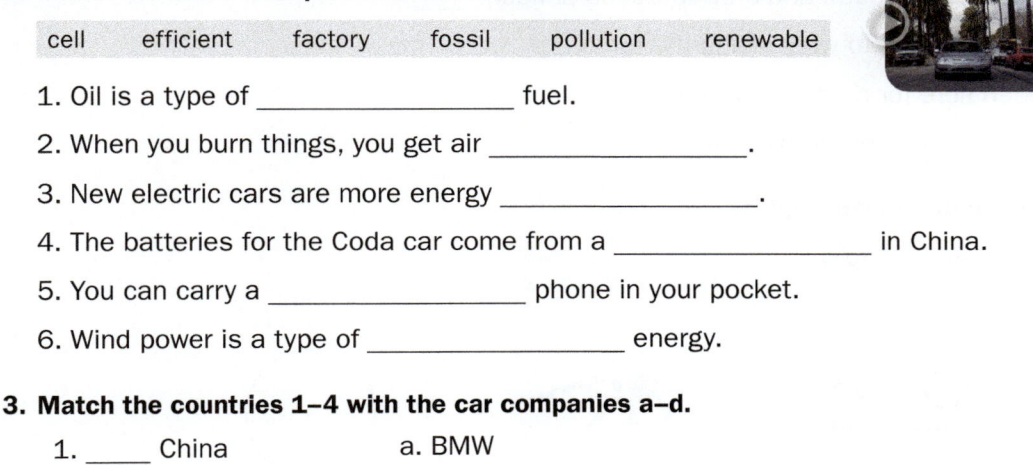

| cell | efficient | factory | fossil | pollution | renewable |

1. Oil is a type of _____ fuel.
2. When you burn things, you get air _____.
3. New electric cars are more energy _____.
4. The batteries for the Coda car come from a _____ in China.
5. You can carry a _____ phone in your pocket.
6. Wind power is a type of _____ energy.

Discovery EDUCATION
7.4 DRIVING INTO THE FUTURE

3. Match the countries 1–4 with the car companies a–d.

1. _____ China
2. _____ Germany
3. _____ Japan
4. _____ USA

a. BMW
b. Chevy & Ford
c. BYD
d. Nissan

PROJECT

In groups, think of ways you and your classmates can help the environment. Here are some ideas:

- Recycle your old computers and cell phones
- Save energy in your home (turn off lights when you leave the room, take a two-minute shower, unplug appliances when you're not using them)
- Join an environmental group
- Take the bus, ride a bike, or walk to school

Make a presentation and show your ideas to the others in the class. Then ask the class to vote on the best ideas.

Ancient SYMBOLS

CLIL PROJECT

1. **Match the words with the correct definitions.**

   | archeologist | hieroglyphics | skeleton | strap | tomb |

   1. The bones of a human or animal body _____
   2. A person who studies very old places and things _____
   3. Egyptian writing from thousands of years ago _____
   4. A stone structure for a dead body of a person _____
   5. A narrow piece of leather or other strong material. You use it to connect something, like a sandal _____

   Discovery EDUCATION
   9.4 PICTURES WITH MEANING

2. **Watch the video. Number the sentences 1–5 in the order that you hear them.**

   a. Mansour Bourek is an archeologist. ____
   b. And here's a goose, a leaf, a mouth, and a strap from a sandal. ____
   c. His team of archeologists come to work inside the tomb. ____
   d. This skeleton has been here for over 2,000 years. ____
   e. Ahmed's family lives above one of the biggest tombs. ____

3. **Match the words with the correct hieroglyphics.**

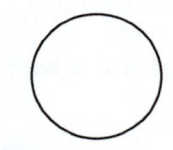

   | goose | hill country | sun | to cry |

   1 _____   2 _____   3 _____   4 _____

   PROJECT

   About 200 years ago, French soldiers discovered an ancient stone in Egypt with a story written on it. Scientists determined that the story was in three different languages: Greek, Demotic script (the common writing used in ancient Egyptian documents), and in hieroglyphics. The scientists knew how to read Greek, so they were able to understand the hieroglyphics! They named the stone the Rosetta Stone.

   Now create your own Rosetta Stone. Write a story about what you think life was like in ancient Egypt. Do research and see if you can translate your story into hieroglyphics.

Irregular verbs

Base Verb	Simple Past	Past Participle
babysit	babysat	babysat
be	was, were	been
become	became	become
begin	began	begun
bleed	bled	bled
blow	blew	blown
break	broke	broken
bring	brought	brought
build	built	built
burn	burned/burnt	burned/burnt
buy	bought	bought
catch	caught	caught
choose	chose	chosen
come	came	come
cost	cost	cost
cut	cut	cut
deal	dealt	dealt
dive	dived/dove	dived
do	did	done
draw	drew	drawn
dream	dreamed/dreamt	dreamed/dreamt
drink	drank	drunk
drive	drove	driven
eat	ate	eaten
fall	fell	fallen
feel	felt	felt
fight	fought	fought
find	found	found
fly	flew	flown
forget	forgot	forgotten
freeze	froze	frozen
get	got	gotten
give	gave	given
go	went	gone
grow	grew	grown
hang	hung	hung
have	had	had
hear	heard	heard
hide	hid	hidden
hit	hit	hit
hold	held	held
hurt	hurt	hurt
keep	kept	kept

Base Verb	Simple Past	Past Participle
know	knew	known
leave	left	left
let	let	let
lie	lay	lain
lose	lost	lost
make	made	made
mean	meant	meant
meet	met	met
pay	paid	paid
put	put	put
read	read	read
ride	rode	ridden
ring	rang	rung
rise	rose	risen
run	ran	run
say	said	said
see	saw	seen
sell	sold	sold
send	sent	sent
set	set	set
show	showed	shown
shut	shut	shut
sing	sang	sung
sit	sat	sat
sleep	slept	slept
speak	spoke	spoken
spend	spent	spent
spread	spread	spread
stand	stood	stood
steal	stole	stolen
stick	stuck	stuck
swim	swam	swum
take	took	taken
teach	taught	taught
tell	told	told
think	thought	thought
throw	threw	thrown
understand	understood	understood
wake	woke	woken
wear	wore	worn
win	won	won
write	wrote	written

Credits

The authors and publishers acknowledge the following sources of copyright material and are grateful for the permissions granted. While every effort has been made, it has not always been possible to identify the sources of all the material used, or to trace all copyright holders. If any omissions are brought to our notice, we will be happy to include the appropriate acknowledgements on reprinting.

p. 2-3 (B/G): Shutterstock Images/John McCormick; p. 3 (a): Alamy/©Piero Cruciatti; p. 3 (b): Shutterstock Images/egd; p. 3 (c): Shutterstock Images/James BO Insogna; p. 3 (d): Alamy/©Matthew Chattle; p. 3 (e): Alamy/©blickwinkel; p. 3 (f): Shutterstock Images/Igumnova Irina; p. 3 (g): Getty Images/Sam Yeh/AFP; p. 4 (B/G): Shutterstock Images/Kathriba; p. 4 (TL): Getty Images/National Geographic; p. 4 (TR): Alamy/©RIA Novosti; p. 5 (CL): Alamy/©Jeff Schultz/Alaska Stock; p. 6 (B/G): Shutterstock Images/Yulia Glam; p. 7 (CR): Shutterstock Images/Andrey_Popov; p. 8 (L): Alamy/©Roy Johnson; p. 9 (TR): Shutterstock Images/Raymona Pooler; p. 10 (TL): Alamy/©Chris Howarth/South Atlantic; p. 10 (B/G): Shutterstock Images/Freesoulproduction; p. 11 (1): Shutterstock Images/Ashraf Jandali; p.11 (2): Shutterstock Images/Rarach; p.11 (3): Alamy/©Barry Diomede; p. 11 (4): Shutterstock Images/OHishiapply; p. 11 (5): Alamy/©EB Images/Blend Images; p. 11 (6): Alamy/©Paul Maguire; p. 12-13 (B/G): Corbis/JGI/Jamie Grill; p. 13 (a): Shutterstock Images/Syda Productions; p. 13 (b): Alamy/©Tetra Images; p. 13 (c): Alamy/©Kuttig – People; p. 13 (e): Shutterstock Images/Pressmaster; p.13 (g): Alamy/©Juice Images; p. 13 (f): Shutterstock Images/Masson; p. 13 (g): Superstock/age footstock; p. 13 (i): Getty Images/Image Source; p. 13 (i): Shutterstock Images/kuznetcov_konstantin; p. 14 (TL): Shutterstock Images/Lasse Kristensen; p. 15 (TR): Alamy/©PCN Photography; p. 16 (TR): Shutterstock Images/Lucky Business; p. 16 (a): Shutterstock Images/Ruslan Guzov; p. 16 (b): Shutterstock Images/Dragon Images;p. 16 (c): Shutterstock Images/Pressmaster; p. 16 (d): Shutterstock Images/Creatista; p. 16 (e): Shutterstock Images/Photographee.eu;p. 16 (f): Getty Images/Nick Dolding; p. 16 (g): Alamy/©Bjorn Andren/Robert Matton AB; p. 17 (TR): Shutterstock Images/Alexander Raths; p. 18 (TL): Alamy/©Kumar Sriskandan; p. 18 (BL): Corbis/Hill Street Studios/Blend Images; p. 19 (TR): Alamy/©Sverre Haugland; p. 20 (B/G): Shutterstock Images/William Perugini; p. 20 (T): Alamy/©AJSH Photograph; p. 21 (BR): Shutterstock Images/Andreasnikolas; p. 22-23 (B/G): Alamy/©JL Images; p. 23 (a): Alamy/©Jeff Gilbert; p. 23 (b): Alamy/©Michele and Tom Grimm;p. 23 (c):Alamy/©Arco Images GmbH; p. 23 (d): Alamy/©Paul Lovichi Photography; p. 23 (e): Alamy/©eddie linssen; p. 23 (f): Alamy/©Nagelestock.com; p. 23 (g): Alamy/©Tony French; p. 23 (h): Alamy/©Andrew Aitchison; p. 23 (i): Shutterestock/Grynold; p. 23 (j): Alamy/©Christina K; p. 24 (B/G): Shutterstock Images/Jag_cz; p. 24 (T): Alamy/©Kevin Britland; p. 25 (BL): Alamy/©LWA/Dann Tardif/Blend Images; p. 26 (TL): Alamy/©i stage; p. 26 (a): Alamy/©Aki; p. 26 (b): Shutterstock Images/Furtseff; p. 26 (c): Shutterstock Images/Vereshchagin Dmitry; p. 26 (d): Shutterstock/Christian Bertrand; p. 26 (e): Shutterstock Images/mphot; p. 26 (f): Shutterstock Images/Dario Sabljak; p. 26 (g): Shutterstock Images/Chromakey; p. 26 (h): Alamy/©lem; p. 26 (i):Shutterstock Images/vvoe; p. 26 (j): Shutterstock Images/ Visun Khankasem; p. 27 (TR): Alamy/©Graham Salter/Lebrecht Music & Arts; p. 28 (L): Shutterstock Images/Warren Goldswain; p. 29 (TL): Alamy/©david pearson; p. 30 (TR): Alamy/©ZUMA Press, Inc.; p. 30 (BL): Shutterstock Images/Fluke samed; p. 32-33 (B/G): Getty Images/Vetta/Scott Hailstone; p. 33 (a): Alamy/©J.R.Bale; p. 33 (b): Superstock/age footstock; p. 33 (c): Getty Images/Ken Chernus/Taxi; p. 33 (d): Shutterstock Images/Greg Epperson; p. 33 (e): Alamy/©PhotoEdit; p. 33 (f): Alamy/©Age Fotostock Spain S.L.; p. 33 (g): Alamy/©Dmitry Burlakov; p. 33 (h): Shutterstock Images/PhotoSky; p. 33 (i): Alamy/©ZUMA Press, Inc.; p. 34 (TL): Alamy/©Gaspar Avila; p. 34 (BL): Alamy/©ZUMA Press, Inc.; p. 35 (CR): Shutterstock Images/Tetra Images; p. 36 (TL): Getty Images/Philip and Karen Smith; p. 36 (BL): Alamy/©Westend61 GmbH; p. 37 (TR): Alamy/©Cultura; p. 38 (TL): Alamy/©Hemis; p. 38 (CL): Shutterstock Images/Strahil Dimitrov; p. 38 (BL): Shutterstock Images/Graphichead; p. 39 (TR): Corbis/Radius Images; p. 40 (T): Shutterstock Images/Pichugin Dmitry; p. 40 (a): Shutterstock Images/Bildagentur Zoonar GmbH; p. 40 (b): Alamy/©Howard Davies; p. 40 (c): Robert Harding Picture Library/Stuart Black/AgeFotostock; p. 40 (d): Alamy/©John Elk III; p. 40 (e): Shutterstock Images/Konrad Mostert; p. 40 (B/G): Shutterstock Images/Sasapee; p. 42-43 (B/G): Corbis/2/Andrew Bret Wallis/Ocean; p. 43 (a): Shutterstock Images/Dmitrijs Bindemanis; p. 43 (b): Shutterstock Images/Matteo photos; p. 43 (c): Alamy/©Robin Beckham/BEEPstock; p. 43 (d): Shutterstock Images/Jayakumar; p. 43 (e): Shutterstock Images/Jag_cz; p. 43 (f): Shutterstock Images/Lisa F. Young; p. 43 (g): Alamy/©Phil Degginger; p. 43 (h): Shutterstock Images/Blend Images; p. 44 (TR): Shutterstock Images/Andresr; p. 44 (1): UNIVERSAL/THE KOBAL COLLECTION/BOLAND, JASIN; p. 44 (2): UNIVERSAL/THE KOBAL COLLECTION/MOSELEY, MELISSA; p. 44 (3): HAMMER FILM PRODUCTIONS/THE KOBAL COLLECTION; p. 44 (4): MIRAMAX/THE KOBAL COLLECTION/FOREMAN, RICHARD; p. 44 (5): 20TH CENTURY FOX/THE KOBAL COLLECTION; p. 44 (6): CODE RED PRODUCTIONS/THE KOBAL COLLECTION; p. 44 (7): NEW REGENCY PICTURES/THE KOBAL COLLECTION; p. 46 (TL): Alamy/©Gunter Marx; p. 46 (BL): Alamy/©Ruby; p. 46 (BL): Alamy/©GeoStills; p. 47 (TR): Alamy/©Gunter Marx; p. 48 (B/G): Shutterstock Images/Kamira; p. 49 (TR): Shutterstock Images/Pincasso; p. 50 (TR): Alamy/©Adrian Turner; p. 50 (B/G): Shutterstock Images/Shchipkova Elena; p. 51 (TR): Shutterstock Images/Jacek Chabraszewski; p. 52-53 (B/G): Corbis/Herbert Meyrl/Westend61; p. 54-55 (B/G): Getty Images/Kevin Spreekmeester; p. 56 (TC): Shutterstock Images/Feng Yu; p. 57 (B): Alamy/©Agencja Fotograficzna Caro; p. 58 (CL): Alamy/©Denise Hager Catchlight Visual Services; p. 58 (TL): Shutterstock Images/Sean Locke Photography; p. 59 (CR): Alamy/©Richard G. Bingham II; p. 60 (TL): Shutterstock Images/IPranoffee; p. 60 (BL): Getty Images/Chris Schmidt; p. 60 (BC): Alamy/©Tony Cordoza; p. 60 (BR): Alamy/©Marjorie Kamys Cotera/Bob Daemmrich Photography; p. 61 (TL): Shutterstock Images/Ermolaev Alexander; p. 62 (B/G): Shutterstock Images/Albund; p. 62 (TL): Alamy/©Picture Partners; p. 62 (TR): Alamy/©Denise Hager Catchlight Visual Services; p. 63 (TR): Shutterstock Images/Dmitry Kalinovsky; p. 64-65 (B/G): Shutterstock Images/Albachiaraa; p. 65 (a): Shutterstock Images/Lanych; p. 65 (b): Shutterstock Images/Luchi_a; p. 65 (c): Shutterstock Images/K.Miri Photography; p. 65 (d): Shutterstock Images/Coprid; p. 65 (e): Shutterstock Images/Stockphoto Graf; p. 65 (f): Shutterstock Images/FreeBirdPhotos; p. 65 (g): Shutterstock Images/DigitalMagus; p. 65 (h): Shutterstock Images/Praisaeng; p. 65 (i): Shutterstock Images/Vadim Ratnikov; p. 65 (j): Shutterstock Images/Coprid; p. 66 (TL): Shutterstock Images/John Kasawa; p. 66 (TL): Alamy/©jay goebel; p. 67 (CR): Alamy/©eye35.pix; p. 68 (TL): Alamy/©Bubbles Photolibrary; p. 69 (CR): Shutterstock Images/Minerva Studio; p. 70 (BC): Shutterstock Images/Pressmaster;p.70 (BR): Alamy/©PhotoAlto sas; p. 70 (TL): Alamy/©Jim West; p. 71 (TL): Alamy/©Purestock; p. 72 (TR): Alamy/©Justin Hannaford; p. 72 (CR): Alamy/©Chris Cooper-Smith; p. 72 (T): Shutterstock Images/CoolR; p. 72 (B): Shutterstock Images/Imagevixen; p. 73 (1): Alamy/©Cristina Fumi Photography; p. 73 (2): Shutterstock Images/Felix Rohan; p. 73 (3): Shutterstock Images/Alex Staroseltsev; p. 73 (4): Shutterstock Images/MNI; p. 73 (5): Shutterstock Images/Elena Blokhina; p. 73 (6): Shutterstock Images/Mama_mia; p. 74-75 (B/G): Corbis/Wave; p. 75 (a):Shutterstock Images/Lafoto; p. 75 (b): Shutterstock Images/st.djura; p. 75 (c): Shutterstock Images/Morten Normann Almeland; p. 75 (d): Shutterstock Images/Vaju Ariel; p. 75 (e): Shutterstock Images/Gts; p. 75 (f): Alamy/©Zacarias Pereira Da Mata; p. 75 (g): Shutterstock Images/chaoss; p. 75 (h): Shutterstock Images/jo Crebbin; p. 75 (i): Alamy/©Avico Ltd; p. 76 (T): Alamy/©Keith J Smith; p. 77 (TR): Shutterstock Images/Sekar B; p. 78 (T): Alamy/©Paul Mayall Australia; p. 78 (a): Shutterstock Images/Gresei; p. 78 (b): Shutterstock Images/Brian A Jackson; p. 78 (c): Shutterstock Images/Nikitabuida; p. 78 (d): Alamy/©BSIP SA; p. 78 (e): Shutterstock Images/Tony740607; p. 78 (f): Shutterstock Images/Grynold; p. 78 (g): Shutterstock Images/Tatiana Popova; p. 78 (h): Shutterstock Images/Ti Santi; p. 78 (i): Alamy/©D.Hurst; p. 79 (TR): Getty Images/Nacivet; p. 80 (TL): Shutterstock Images/Lamreal-kobzeva; p. 80 (CL): Shutterstock Images/scyther5; p. 80 (BL): Shutterstock Images/Ervin Monn; p. 81 (T): Alamy/©Blend Images; p. 82 (TR): Corbis/Jim Reed/Jim Reed Photography - Severe &; p. 82 (T): Shutterstock Images/Minerva Studio; p. 82 (B/G): Shutterstock Images/Minerva Studio; p. 83 (BL): Shutterstock Images/Gorillaimages; p. 84-85 (B/G): Alamy/©Science Photo Library; p. 85 (CR): Alamy/©JGI/Jamie Grill/Blend Images; p. 86 (T): Shutterstock Images/Littleny; p. 87 (BR): Getty Images/Mark Bowden; p. 88 (a): Shutterstock Images/Syda Productions; p. 88 (b): Alamy/©Blend Images; p. 88 (c): Getty Images/Yellow Dog Productions; p. 88 (d): Getty Images/iStockphoto; p. 89 (CR): Getty Images/Debra Roets/Le Club Symphonie; p. 90 (TL): Shutterstock Images/Goodluz; p. 91 (TR): Shutterstock Images/Stephen Coburn; p. 92 (TL): Alamy/©Liquid Light; p. 92 (CL): Alamy/©Kathy deWitt; p. 92 (BL): Alamy/©Tim Graham; p. 92 (B): Shutterstock Images/FrameAngel; p. 94-95 (B/G): Corbis/Pete Saloutos/Image Source; p. 96 (TL): Shutterstock Images/Arieliona; p. 97 (TR): Alamy/©Redsnapper; p. 98 (TL): Alamy/©Steve Lindridge; p. 99 (CR): Alamy/©Paul/F1online Digitale Bildagentur GmbH; p. 100 (TL): Alamy/©Robert Harding World Imagery; p. 100 (BL): Alamy/©Bob Daemmrich; p. 101 (TL): Alamy/©Steve Skjold; p. 102 (T, B/G): Alamy/©Zuma Press; p. 104-105 (B/G): Corbis/Marc Dozier; p. 120 (BR): Alamy/©The Print Collector; Back cover: Shutterstock Images/fluke samed.

Front cover photography by Alamy/©Martin Strmiska.

The publishers are grateful to the following illustrators:
Q2A Media Services, Inc. p. 6, 116, 120; Martin Sanders p. 28.

All video stills by kind permission of:
Discovery Communications, LLC 2015: p. 2 (1, 3, 4), 5, 10, 11, 12 (1, 3), 15, 20, 22 (1, 3, 4), 25, 30, 31, 32 (1, 3), 35, 40, 42 (1, 3, 4), 45, 50, 51, 54 (1, 3), 57, 62, 64 (1, 3, 4), 67, 72, 73, 74 (1, 3), 77, 82, 84 (1, 3, 4), 87, 92, 93, 94 (1, 3), 97, 102, 116, 117, 118, 119, 120; Cambridge University Press: p. 2 (2), 8, 12 (2), 18, 22 (2), 28, 32 (2), 38, 42 (2), 48, 54 (2), 60, 64 (2), 70, 74 (2), 80, 84 (2), 90, 94 (2), 100.